The Doha Round and Financial Services Negotiations

The Doha Round and Financial Services Negotiations

Sydney J. Key

The AEI Press

Publisher for the American Enterprise Institute

WASHINGTON, D.C.

2003

Available in the United States from the AEI Press, c/o Client Distribution Services, 193 Edwards Drive, Jackson, TN 38301. To order, call toll free: 1-800-343-4499. Distributed outside the United States by arrangement with Eurospan, 3 Henrietta Street, London WC2E 8LU, England.

Library of Congress Cataloging-in-Publication Data
Key, Sydney J.
    The Doha round and financial services negotiations / Sydney J. Key.
      p. cm.
    Includes bibliographical references and index.
    ISBN 0-8447-4182-5 (pbk.)
    1. Financial services industry—Law and legislation 2. Foreign trade regulation. I. Title

    K1066.K49 2003
    343'.087—dc 22

                                             2003063553

1 3 5 7 9 10 8 6 4 2

Printed in the United States of America

Contents

—◦◦◦—

Foreword

In advanced industrial economies, the services sector accounts for a substantial portion of each nation's gross domestic product. Despite the increasing importance of trade in services, the General Agreement on Trade in Services (GATS), which was negotiated during the 1986–94 Uruguay Round and entered into force in January 1995, marked the first time that rules for opening markets in services were included in the multilateral trading system. The GATS called for periodic negotiating rounds, beginning no later than 2000, to achieve further liberalization of trade in services. Serious individual sector negotiations, however, did not shift into high gear until a comprehensive new round of multilateral trade negotiations was launched at the November 2001 ministerial meeting of the World Trade Organization (WTO) in Doha, Qatar.

The American Enterprise Institute is engaged in a research project to focus on the latest round of trade negotiations on services. Mounted in conjunction with the Kennedy School of Government at Harvard University, the Brookings Institution, and the Coalition of Service Industries Research and Education Foundation, the project entails analysis of individual economic sectors: financial services; accounting; insurance; electronic commerce; energy; air freight and air cargo; airline passenger services; and entertainment and culture. Each study identifies major barriers to trade liberalization in the sector under scrutiny and assesses policy options for trade negotiators and interested private sector participants.

AEI would like to acknowledge the following donors for their generous support of the trade-in-services project: American Express Company; American International Group; CIGNA Corporation; FedEx Corporation; Mastercard International; the Motion Picture Association of America; and the Mark Twain Institute. I emphasize, however, that the conclusions and recommendations of the individual studies are solely those of authors.

Issues for the Financial Services Negotiations

In this study, Sydney J. Key analyzes the role of the GATS and the WTO in the liberalization and regulation of the financial services sector and identifies six broad goals for the financial services negotiations in the Doha round. What makes her analysis unique is that she integrates the two very different perspectives of trade policy and financial regulatory policy. Throughout the study, Key emphasizes the complementary and mutually reinforcing relationship between efforts to open markets under the GATS and the intensive ongoing international work on strengthening domestic financial systems, including prudential regulation and supervision.

The study examines the role of the GATS and the WTO in relation to what Key characterizes as the three pillars of liberalization necessary to achieve "international contestability of markets": (1) opening markets to foreign services and service suppliers through GATS commitments to provide "national treatment" and "market access"; (2) implementing domestic structural reforms that would eliminate nondiscriminatory structural barriers to trade in financial services; and (3) liberalizing capital movements. Key explains that the GATS deals with third-pillar liberalization only insofar as it affects countries' specific commitments to liberalize trade in services; in general, liberalization of capital movements is a matter of concern for the International Monetary Fund (IMF).

Key emphasizes the importance of focusing on fundamental first-pillar liberalization in the Doha round financial services negotiations and sets forth four first-pillar goals: first, binding in the GATS existing and ongoing liberalization that provides market access and national treatment; second, removing remaining barriers to national treatment and market access and binding the resulting liberalization; third, narrowing or withdrawing the broad exemptions that some countries have taken from the most favored nation (MFN) obligation of the GATS; and, fourth, using an incremental approach for cross-border services that combines strengthening GATS commitments and achieving greater liberalization in practice.

How far should the Doha round financial services negotiations extend into the realm of second-pillar liberalization? Like other authors in this series, Key grapples with the role of the GATS with regard to the domestic structural reform needed to reduce or eliminate nondiscriminatory structural barriers to trade in services. Key believes that the Doha round financial services negotiations should proceed selectively by concentrating on the areas in which the GATS and the WTO have a comparative advantage. She singles out two particularly important second-pillar goals for the Doha round financial services negotiations: developing stronger GATS disciplines on regulatory transparency; and removing barriers to "effective market access" and binding the resulting liberalization.

Key argues that GATS rules on transparency in developing and applying regulations, together with the closely related principle of procedural "fairness" in applying regulations, would not only help eliminate barriers created by opaque and unfair regulatory procedures but also help ensure that a country does not use its regulatory process to undermine its commitments to national treatment and market access. Key explains how GATS rules on transparency in financial services regulation could both complement and build upon the work on transparency that is part of international efforts to strengthen domestic financial systems.

The other second-pillar goal set forth by Key involves anticompetitive domestic regulatory measures that cannot be justified on prudential grounds and serve primarily to keep foreign financial firms from competing in host-country markets by making entry impractical or too costly—thereby denying them "effective market access." Key explains that identifying barriers to effective market access that could be negotiated in the Doha round requires a country's trading partners to determine whether, in practice, a host country's measures keep foreign firms from competing in its markets and whether a "critical mass" of regulators believes that the measures are inappropriate for prudential purposes. She points out, however, that even if the prevalent regulatory view is that the measures cannot be justified on prudential grounds, host-country regulators must be persuaded to accept it.

What about barriers to trade in financial services that are created by legitimate prudential measures? Key explains the importance of the "prudential carve-out" for domestic regulation in the GATS Annex on Financial

Services: it ensures the GATS will not interfere with the ability of national authorities to exercise their responsibilities for prudential regulation and supervision to protect consumers of financial services and to promote the integrity and stability of the financial system. She notes that while prudential measures sometimes impose additional requirements on foreign firms, they may also create barriers simply because they differ among countries—that is, financial firms operating on a global basis may often find it burdensome to comply with a multitude of different national rules.

Key identifies two approaches for dealing with barriers created by prudential measures. One would have home-country regulatory authorities convince host-country authorities that their prudential concerns can be addressed with less sweeping requirements. These efforts could take place bilaterally or in various international fora, including the financial services negotiations under the auspices of the WTO, where finance ministries play a major role. A second approach would have home- and host-country authorities negotiate a recognition arrangement. Although the GATS Annex on Financial Services facilitates unilateral or mutual recognition of prudential measures by permitting a departure from the MFN obligation of the GATS for such arrangements, Key explains why the WTO is not the appropriate forum for their negotiation.

In conclusion, Key summarizes the forces affecting the outcome of the Doha round financial services negotiations and the importance of that outcome to the process of financial sector liberalization:

> Success in achieving the financial services goals discussed in this study depends significantly on factors beyond the scope of the negotiations. As the GATS explicitly recognizes, liberalization of trade in financial and other services is an ongoing process. For financial services, this process is being driven in large part by market forces and new technologies. It is also being driven by the growing recognition among policymakers that market opening can benefit host-country consumers of financial services and, at the same time, contribute to the resiliency of domestic financial systems. The development of international minimum standards and codes of good practices for sound financial systems and their implementation by individual

countries provides a strong foundation for moving ahead with further liberalization of trade in financial services. The negotiations in the Doha round can play an important role in helping to accelerate the process of liberalization as well as solidifying its results in the form of binding commitments subject to the WTO dispute settlement mechanism.

CLAUDE BARFIELD
American Enterprise Institute
for Public Policy Research

Acknowledgments

—◦◦◦—

The author greatly appreciates the assistance of the many individuals who read all or part of the manuscript and provided valuable comments and suggestions in their areas of expertise. She would like to thank Alistair Abercrombie, Claude Barfield, Nicholas Bayne, Stijn Claessens, Steven Fabry, Bernard M. Hoekman, Cecilia Klein, Masamichi Kono, Robert D. Kramer, Patrick Macrory, Ann Main, Marilyn L. Muench, Kathleen M. O'Day, Patrick Pearson, Mary S. Podesta, Amelia Porges, Peter E.W. Russell, Hal S. Scott, Richard E. Self, Jonathan D. Stoloff, and T. Whittier Warthin for reading the manuscript in its entirety. She would also like to thank Peter Berz, Barbara J. Bouchard, James M. Boughton, David T. Coe, Kenneth Freiberg, Ralph Kozlow, Ross B. Leckow, Michael D. Mann, Juan A. Marchetti, Peter K. Morrison, William A. Ryback, David Strongin, Mark W. Swinburne, Andrew Velthaus, and Obie G. Whichard for reading drafts, and often redrafts, of particular sections. Finally, the author would like to thank Juyne Linger for her work in editing the manuscript.

1

Introduction

—⟨♦♦♦⟩—

The General Agreement on Trade in Services (GATS), the first global trade agreement to cover financial and other services, is an important new element in the international framework for liberalization and regulation of the financial sector. Participation in the GATS, however, does not necessarily mean that a country has made strong commitments to open its markets to foreign services and service providers. Indeed, the strength of commitments varies substantially among countries. The GATS therefore requires periodic negotiating rounds on financial and other services to improve commitments and thus achieve "a progressively higher level of liberalization."[1]

The GATS was negotiated in the Uruguay Round, which was launched in 1986 and formally concluded in April 1994.[2] Financial services, however, was one of several sectors for which negotiations on specific commitments were extended, and final agreement was not reached until December 1997.[3] In 2000, in accordance with the deadline established by the GATS for initiating a new round of services negotiations, work began again on financial and other services. This occurred despite the failure of the Seattle ministerial meeting of the World Trade Organization (WTO) in December 1999 to launch a comprehensive new round of trade negotiations. Subsequently, at the Doha ministerial meeting in November 2001, WTO members reached agreement on an agenda for comprehensive multilateral trade negotiations that incorporated the so-called "built-in" agenda for financial and other services.[4] The ministerial declaration set January 1, 2005, as the deadline for completing the Doha round; the declaration called for the next ministerial meeting, subsequently scheduled for September 2003 in Cancún, to assess progress and provide any necessary political guidance.[5]

1

For financial services liberalization, four aspects of the GATS and the WTO are particularly significant:

First, the WTO is a multilateral forum in which the primary goal is reducing or eliminating trade barriers to promote competitive markets and thereby support economic growth and development. The new prominence of this goal at the multilateral level complements the intensive work on strengthening domestic financial systems in a variety of other international fora, ranging from institutions such as the International Monetary Fund (IMF) to specialized bodies such as the Basel Committee on Banking Supervision.[6] Indeed, the efforts to liberalize trade in financial services and the efforts to strengthen domestic financial systems, including prudential regulation and supervision, are mutually reinforcing. In addition, the WTO is a forum in which all members have the opportunity to participate on an equal basis. Multilateral trade agreements are negotiated in the WTO without the "conditionality" that links IMF or World Bank financial assistance to the implementation of specific policy measures by a borrowing country.[7] In principle, therefore, GATS commitments to liberalization have "domestic ownership"—that is, they reflect a country's recognition of the need for policy reform—a quality that the IMF has found to be a crucial determinant of the success of its programs.[8]

Second, the GATS provides a mechanism for parties to undertake legally binding commitments subject to enforcement under the WTO dispute settlement mechanism. A GATS commitment is permanent in that it cannot be withdrawn without compensation of trading partners. Failure to honor a commitment could open a country to a dispute settlement proceeding and, ultimately, WTO-sanctioned retaliatory measures by its trading partners. Thus, backsliding in the face of protectionist domestic political pressures could be extremely costly. As a result, binding even the status quo is extremely important. Moreover, for negotiations that stretch over many years, the "status quo" in the final phase is often different from that at the outset of the negotiations, in part as a result of the negotiating process itself.

Third, the GATS is based on the most-favored-nation (MFN) principle, which precludes discrimination among foreign countries. Under the MFN obligation of the GATS, a WTO member must accord to services and service suppliers of any other member treatment "no less favorable" than the treatment it provides to "like" services and service suppliers of the most favored foreign nation.[9] The reach of the MFN obligation is very broad because it applies to all measures affecting trade in services that are covered by the GATS, not just those for which a member has made specific commitments to liberalization.[10] Although the GATS does allow members to enter into economic integration agreements—such as the Treaty establishing the European Community (EC Treaty)[11] and the North American Free Trade Agreement (NAFTA)—without extending the benefits of the agreements to all WTO members, it establishes stringent criteria for an agreement to qualify for this exception.[12] If a WTO member undertakes liberalizing measures in connection with services obligations in an agreement that does not meet the criteria, it must apply the measures to all WTO members on an MFN basis.[13]

Fourth, the GATS negotiating process can itself have a positive impact on domestic policymaking, particularly in emerging market economies and other developing countries. Governments that participate in the negotiations are forced to account to their trading partners for the barriers they impose and to explore the possibility of overcoming domestic political constraints to reduce or eliminate those barriers. A continuing challenge for the trading partners is to use the GATS negotiating process to provide support for and to harness political and market forces that are creating pressures for liberalization within a host country. In this regard, a country's "readiness" for reform is critical. Thus, the outcome of the GATS process depends heavily on factors beyond its purview.

The next chapter of this study presents a brief discussion of the international provision of financial services and their coverage by the GATS. The third chapter provides a framework for analyzing the role of the GATS and the WTO in liberalization and regulation of the financial sector. The fourth chapter focuses on the barriers to national treatment and market access that need to be addressed in the financial services negotiations in the Doha round. The fifth chapter examines nondiscriminatory structural barriers and identifies certain areas of domestic structural reform that could usefully be dealt with in the GATS negotiations. The final chapter presents the conclusions of this study.

2

International Trade in Financial Services

⟜∿⟞

The financial sector is a critical component of a nation's economy: It not only contributes directly to output and employment but also provides an essential infrastructure for the functioning of the entire economy. The financial system serves as a channel through which savings can be mobilized and used to finance investment and, at the same time, facilitates transactions necessary for internal and external trade. It also helps to manage risks and reduce so-called information asymmetries between providers and users of funds.[1] For these reasons, a sound and efficient financial system is imperative for economic growth and development. A sound financial system also increases the resiliency of a nation's economy, thereby helping it to withstand external shocks such as movements in exchange rates or a major increase in global interest rates.

International trade in financial services—together with enhanced prudential regulation and supervision and other basic structural reforms—can play an important role in helping countries build financial systems that are more competitive and efficient, and therefore more stable. Financial services trade can enhance capital market efficiency; improve the quality, availability, and pricing of financial services; stimulate innovation through the dissemination of new technologies, know-how, and skills; and promote the use of international good practices in areas such as accounting, risk management, and disclosure of financial information.[2] The rapid growth of trade in financial services in recent years reflects a combination of economic, technological, and regulatory factors.[3] These include new and expanding markets in developing and transition economies, technological advances, and progress in reducing or eliminating a variety of host-country barriers (see chapter 3).

4

Trade in services, as defined in the GATS, includes services provided across borders and through foreign direct investment. The cross-border provision of services—for example, the provision of financial services from an office located in one country to residents of another country—is broadly analogous to trade in goods.[4] By contrast, foreign direct investment involves the establishment of a commercial presence, such as a branch or subsidiary within a host country.[5] The GATS approach of defining international trade to include services provided to host-country customers through the establishment and operation of a commercial presence differs from the approach used for balance-of-payments purposes, in which once a local branch or subsidiary has been established, the services it provides to host-country customers are treated as domestic.[6]

In this study, the term "financial services" refers to financial services other than insurance, which is the subject of another study in this series.[7] Although the GATS definition of financial services encompasses both "insurance and insurance-related services" and "banking and other financial services (excluding insurance),"[8] they have been negotiated and listed in the financial services schedules as separate subsectors.[9] These subsectors are, however, closely linked. Many of the major commercial and investment banks operating internationally are part of financial conglomerates that also include firms engaged in insurance underwriting, and banks often engage directly in insurance brokerage activities. Moreover, the development of new types of products and instruments is blurring the distinctions between financial subsectors.

Major financial firms now provide a wide range of financial services to customers in other countries. These include commercial banking activities such as lending and deposit-taking; investment banking activities, such as underwriting securities and advising on mergers and acquisitions; trading activities, that is, brokering and dealing in securities and other financial instruments; and asset-management activities, including management of mutual funds and pension funds. Other financial services provided internationally include financial information and data processing services; investment advisory services; payment and money transmission services, including credit cards; settlement and clearing for financial assets; and financial leasing.

Many financial services provided internationally are wholesale in nature; that is, they are provided to "sophisticated" customers such as corporations and institutions, other financial services firms, and wealthy individuals.[10] Both foreign direct investment and cross-border supply are important means of providing wholesale financial services. In the banking sector, when wholesale services are provided through establishment of a commercial presence, direct branches of the foreign bank—if permitted by host-country regulation—are usually a more efficient form of organization than subsidiaries. Unlike subsidiaries, branches are not separately incorporated in the host country and operate using the firm's consolidated worldwide capital (but see chapter 4 regarding lending limits based on branch capital-equivalency requirements).

E-Finance

Technological advances have long had a major impact on the conduct of wholesale financial activities. Business-to-business electronic transactions *within* the financial sector have been used for more than two decades, both domestically and internationally. Financial firms have also provided online services to nonfinancial firms over closed proprietary networks for a number of years. Widespread access to the open network technology of the Internet, however, offers a whole new range of possibilities to provide services to a much broader base of customers at substantially lower costs. As a result, online services provided to wholesale customers—both within and across national borders—are growing rapidly. This growth includes not only traditional financial services but also new types of services designed to facilitate business-to-business e-commerce activities.[11]

The same technological and cost-saving possibilities exist for the provision of electronic banking and other financial services to retail customers. *Within* some countries, the provision of some types of financial services over the Internet and through web-enabled technologies, such as mobile telephony, is expanding dramatically. Prominent examples include discount brokerage and mutual funds in the United States, and banking services in Finland, Norway, and Sweden.[12] The *cross-border* provision of financial services to retail customers over the Internet, however, is still in its infancy. In general, the international provision of retail financial services still takes place primarily through locally incorporated subsidiaries.[13] Indeed, a number of banks are now using their host-country subsidiaries as a base from which to provide electronic banking services to host-country retail customers.

The lack of widespread development of cross-border retail banking and other financial services—through the Internet or more traditional methods—reflects host-country regulatory requirements aimed at ensuring adequate consumer protection, consumer preferences, and tax considerations. Some countries actually require the establishment of a commercial presence to provide retail financial services. Even when regulatory requirements for cross-border services involve nondiscriminatory application of host-country prudential standards, firms operating on a global basis may have difficulty meeting a multitude of different national requirements. Perhaps even more important, consumers may prefer dealing with a local commercial presence, particularly because redress against a local establishment is usually readily available through the domestic legal system. In addition, in a number of countries, consumers receive more favorable tax treatment on financial products that are provided through locally incorporated entities.[14]

Modes of Supply

In an effort to include all of the ways in which services are provided internationally, the GATS defines "trade in services" in terms of four so-called modes of supply. Mode 1 and mode 2 cover services provided across borders; for financial services, the distinction between these two modes is not always clear. Mode 3 covers services provided through establishment of a commercial presence—that is, through foreign direct investment, a term that is not used in the GATS. Mode 4 covers services provided through the temporary presence of "natural persons," which includes nonlocal employees of a foreign service provider. The GATS uses modes of supply not only to define the scope of its coverage but also as the basis for specific commitments to liberalization that WTO members undertake.

Services Provided across Borders. In this study, the term "cross-border services" is used broadly without attempting to assign a geographic location to the transaction. Thus, this study does not attempt to determine whether a transaction "takes place" in the country of the service provider or in the country of the customer. For example, a cross-border financial services transaction could be carried out in a number of different ways: (a) a representative of, say, a foreign bank might visit the country of the customer to arrange a loan; (b) the customer might travel abroad to visit the office of the foreign bank; or (c) the transaction might take place via telephone, fax , or, increasingly, the Internet, which, in this context, is simply another technological means of delivering the service.[15]

The GATS, however, distinguishes between services provided to nonresidents "from" the country of the service supplier (mode 1 or cross-border supply) and services provided "in" the country of the service supplier (mode 2 or consumption abroad). Usually—but as currently defined by the GATS, not necessarily—mode 2 involves physical movement of the consumer, such as the movement that occurs in tourism.[16] For financial services, however, the line dividing these two modes of supply is not always clear, especially in the case of example (c) in the previous paragraph. Indeed, because financial services are intangible, assigning a geographic site to their provision across borders is difficult and often arbitrary and will become more so as the importance of e-finance increases.

From a regulatory perspective, a major issue is whether, and to what extent, the rules of the host country—that is, the country of the customer—are applied to the cross-border transaction.[17] Suppose, for example, that employees of a foreign bank visit the host country to arrange cross-border loans. Even when the host country does not have a regulatory framework in place for cross-border banking services, host-country bank regulators sometimes look at factors, such as the frequency and duration of visits and the permanence of the host-country infrastructure for the visiting employees, to determine whether, for regulatory purposes, the cross-border activity rises to the level of a host-country office.[18]

Or suppose that a foreign broker-dealer solicits host-country customers to purchase securities. Securities regulators often use solicitation—in addition to the actual conduct of business with domestic residents—as a criterion for determining whether the foreign firm is subject to host-country broker-dealer registration requirements.[19] In response to the increasing use of the Internet by the securities industry, a number of regulators also examine factors such as whether a web site is being used to target host-country customers (see chapter 4).[20] Besides regulatory jurisdiction, another important jurisdictional issue arises in the event of a dispute; here the question is which country's courts have jurisdiction to try the case and which country's laws apply.[21]

Foreign Direct Investment. The inclusion of foreign direct investment in the GATS reflects its importance as a way of providing services internationally.[22] By contrast, the General Agreement on Tariffs and Trade (GATT) does not cover foreign direct investment; for goods, there is only a relatively narrow agreement, negotiated in the Uruguay Round, on trade-related investment measures (TRIMs).[23] Although the GATS includes establishment of a commercial presence as a mode of supply, it does not have a separate framework for investment like that of the NAFTA or the widely used bilateral investment treaties (BITs).[24] These agreements cover portfolio investment as well as direct investment in both goods and services. Moreover, unlike the GATS, they include provisions to ensure the protection of investments—specific rules governing expropriation and compensation, for example—and also provide for arbitration of disputes between private investors and host-country governments.

Presence of Natural Persons. The fourth mode of supply in the GATS, the temporary presence of natural persons, includes the temporary presence in the host country of employees of firms providing services across borders or through a commercial presence. For example, for financial services, this mode of supply covers the presence of nonlocal staff of a host-country branch or subsidiary of a foreign financial firm as well as agents of the firm visiting the host country to facilitate the provision of cross-border services.[25] Although the presence of natural persons is listed as a mode of supply in the GATS, and members can negotiate sector-specific commitments, countries usually make commitments for the temporary presence of natural persons as "horizontal commitments" that apply to all services sectors.[26] For the financial services sector, however, most countries that belong to the Organization for Economic Cooperation and Development (OECD) have incorporated into their schedules a set of commitments allowing the temporary entry of senior managerial personnel and certain types of specialists in association with the establishment of a commercial presence.[27]

3

Liberalization and Regulation

—◦/v/◦—

Policymakers, particularly in emerging market economies, are increasingly recognizing that opening markets to foreign financial firms can benefit both consumers of financial services and the domestic economy as a whole. As noted in chapter 2, the presence of foreign firms can create more competitive and efficient markets for financial services, thereby supporting economic growth and development and contributing to a more resilient domestic financial system. At the same time, however, ensuring adequate prudential regulation and supervision of financial firms and markets, together with other fundamental domestic structural reforms, is essential to obtain the maximum benefits of liberalization while minimizing the risks. Basic structural reforms include increasing transparency and accountability in both the private and public sectors; introducing effective risk management techniques; and developing the institutional infrastructure, such as insolvency laws and appropriate judicial procedures.

Because measures to promote competitive markets and to strengthen domestic financial systems are complementary and mutually reinforcing, the relationship between financial sector liberalization and regulation has two distinct dimensions.[1] On the one hand, liberalization requires reducing or removing anticompetitive regulations that pose unnecessary barriers to trade in services. On the other hand, liberalization requires increasing the strength and quality of certain regulations and, in some areas, introducing new regulations. Thus the process of liberalization involves, inter alia, reaching a consensus on where to draw the line between regulations that are simply anticompetitive barriers to trade—and should therefore be eliminated—and regulations that serve legitimate purposes.

For financial services, the GATS contains a "prudential carve-out" for domestic regulation.[2] In the GATS, the term "prudential" is used broadly to encompass not only measures to promote the integrity and stability of the financial system (as the term has traditionally been used in banking regulation) but also measures designed to protect consumers of financial services. The prudential carve-out, discussed later in this chapter, is designed to ensure that any obligations undertaken or commitments made in the GATS will not interfere with the ability of national authorities to exercise their responsibilities for prudential regulation and supervision. Whether a particular measure is prudential or simply being used to avoid a country's obligations and commitments under the GATS is, however, an issue that could be brought before a WTO dispute settlement panel.

All countries impose certain rules that are clearly prudential. Even if a measure is prudential, however, it may create a barrier to trade in financial services. This could occur because a host country imposes additional prudential requirements on foreign financial firms vis-à-vis their domestic counterparts. Such barriers could also be created simply because prudential rules differ among countries—that is, even if each host country applies the same rules to foreign and domestic firms, financial services firms operating on a global basis often find it burdensome to comply with a multitude of different national prudential rules.

A critical question is whether such barriers could be addressed without jeopardizing prudential goals. Specifically, in what areas and under what conditions might financial services regulators be able and willing to recognize each other's regulations and supervisory practices as being as effective as their own? The GATS is permissive with respect to such recognition arrangements. However, as will be explained in chapters 4 and 5, the WTO is not the appropriate forum for financial services regulators to negotiate recognition of prudential measures.

Three Pillars of Liberalization

"International contestability of markets" refers to the creation of markets that are competitive and efficient on a global basis—a goal that can be achieved by removing all types of barriers to foreign participation in host-country markets.[3] International contestability is, in effect, based on three pillars of liberalization: (1) national treatment and market access; (2) the removal of nondiscriminatory structural barriers, that is, domestic structural reform; and (3) freedom of capital movements.

For financial services, the GATS has so far dealt mainly with the first pillar. An important question for the Doha round is how far the negotiations should extend into the second pillar. The GATS deals with the third pillar only insofar as it affects countries' specific commitments to liberalize trade in services; in general, liberalization of capital movements is a matter of concern for the IMF.[4]

National Treatment and Market Access.[5] The first pillar of international contestability of markets is liberalization aimed at opening markets to foreign services and service suppliers and ensuring that they enjoy substantially the same treatment as their domestic counterparts. Such liberalization requires reducing or removing barriers that discriminate against foreign services and service suppliers with regard to entry and operation in a host-country market. A host country might, for example, discriminate against foreign financial firms by refusing to grant licenses for their branches or subsidiaries; imposing limitations on their ownership position in domestic firms or on their aggregate market share; or prohibiting them from engaging in certain activities that are permissible for their domestic counterparts.

First-pillar liberalization also requires removing various quantitative limitations on the overall provision of services in a host-country market. Although these barriers may not, on their face, be overtly discriminatory, they are typically used to block entry by foreign services and service suppliers. A country might, for example, limit the number of service suppliers in a particular market by restricting the number of new licenses that may be issued or by relying on an economic needs test, which involves an assessment of "needs" in the market by host-country authorities.[6] Because these measures have the effect of imposing some type of quantitative limitation on foreign entry, they are similar to the more overtly discriminatory barriers.

To deal with these first-pillar barriers, the GATS uses the principles of "national treatment" and "market access." Article XVII (National Treatment) relies on a generally accepted definition of national treatment—that is, it requires a host country to treat foreign services and service suppliers no less favorably than "like" domestic services and service suppliers.[7] Barriers to entry or operation that discriminate against foreign services or service suppliers vis-à-vis their domestic counterparts would therefore be inconsistent with national treatment.

The GATS does not attempt to define market access. Instead, Article XVI (Market Access) provides a list of restrictive measures, primarily quantitative, that are typically used by host countries to deny entry to foreign services or service suppliers. A country that does not maintain any of these measures is regarded as providing full market access.[8] The list includes seemingly nondiscriminatory quantitative barriers to entry that apply to both domestic and foreign firms, such as limitations—in the form of numerical quotas or economic needs tests—on the number of service suppliers or their total assets. It also includes quantitative barriers to entry that are clearly discriminatory and thus are also inconsistent with national treatment, such as limitations on foreign ownership interests in domestic firms. As a result, some overlap exists in the national treatment and market access provisions of the GATS—that is, certain measures may be inconsistent with both national treatment and market access.[9] The list of measures in Article XVI also includes restrictions on the type of legal entity through which services may be supplied—for example, requiring establishment of a subsidiary as opposed to a branch.

In the GATS, national treatment and market access are "specific commitments" as opposed to general obligations.[10] As a result, national treatment and market access do not apply across-the-board to all services sectors; instead, they apply *only* to sectors, subsectors, or activities that a WTO member specifically lists in its schedule of commitments.[11] If a member is making only a partial commitment to national treatment or market access *within* a listed sector, subsector, or activity, any limitations must be listed in its schedule.[12] The use of specific commitments for national treatment and market access instead of obligations applicable to all services sectors is in some respects a structural weakness of the GATS.[13] Under a more ambitious approach, such as that used in the NAFTA's services and investment provisions, national treatment and market access would apply in each sector unless an exception was specifically listed in a country's schedule of commitments or one of the public policy exceptions, such as the national security exception, applied.[14]

Nondiscriminatory Structural Barriers. The second pillar of liberalization required for international contestability of markets is aimed at removing nonquantitative and nondiscriminatory structural barriers. Such barriers are associated with national measures that do not discriminate between domestic and foreign services and service suppliers. A second-pillar barrier could arise because a national measure is primarily anticompetitive or fosters anticompetitive behavior by private parties. In some cases, the barrier could be associated with the inadequacy or absence of domestic regulation—for example, the lack of an adequate domestic legal framework for insolvency. A second-pillar barrier could also arise because of differences in national rules, including prudential rules, that make it difficult to conduct operations on a global basis.

Removing second-pillar barriers goes far beyond achieving national treatment and market access. Those principles ensure that foreign services and service suppliers can enter a host-country market *as currently structured* and enjoy equality of competitive opportunities vis-à-vis their domestic counterparts. By contrast, second-pillar liberalization represents an effort to create maximum potential competitive opportunities in a host-country market. Achieving this could require major domestic structural reform. This would necessarily involve some degree of convergence of national regulatory systems, either de facto or through negotiated harmonization.

A longstanding U.S. prohibition on affiliations between banks and insurance companies in the United States, which was repealed in 1999, created a major second-pillar barrier for many years.[15] Indeed, the European Union had found it difficult to accept that a European financial conglomerate that included both a bank and an insurance company could engage in only one of these businesses in the United States. Regardless of whether this nondiscriminatory restriction was primarily anticompetitive or could have been justified as a prudential measure, it nonetheless constituted a barrier to trade in financial services.

Significant second-pillar barriers are often associated with national regulatory regimes for asset-management services.[16] These include across-the-board prohibitions on delegation of functions, such as portfolio management and administrative operations, by the host-country office to a foreign affiliate; extremely strict asset-allocation requirements for a domestic mutual fund or pension fund; and rules that prohibit such funds from investing in foreign securities.[17] While asset management activities raise legitimate prudential concerns about ensuring adequate protection of host-country customers, these types of measures often serve primarily to restrict competition, particularly competition from foreign firms (see chapter 5).

Nondiscriminatory structural barriers to trade in financial services are not limited to financial sector regulation. Barriers in other areas that are particularly important for the effective functioning of the financial services sector, such as lack of adequate frameworks for corporate governance or insolvency, are part of the international work on strengthening domestic financial systems, which is discussed later in this chapter. Ineffective or non-existent competition policy regimes, which could foster anticompetitive behavior by private parties, can also create major second-pillar barriers. Differences in national tax systems are yet another source of second-pillar barriers. Discriminatory treatment of foreign firms under national tax or competition rules, however, would be a first-pillar barrier.[18]

Second-pillar barriers can also arise from a country's administrative procedures—in particular, a lack of regulatory transparency and procedural "fairness." For example, a country might fail to publish all of its laws, regulations, and administrative decisions; administer them in an impartial manner; establish a meaningful procedure for interested parties to comment on proposed regulations; act on applications for licenses within a reasonable period of time; or provide a mechanism for independent review of administrative decisions. Because regulatory transparency and procedural fairness can be extremely effective in ensuring that commitments to market access and national treatment are fully implemented, they constitute an important underpinning of first-pillar liberalization.

The European Union's single-market program represents the most far-reaching effort to date to remove nondiscriminatory structural barriers among a group of nations. Predicated on political agreement on goals for economic liberalization, that effort is being carried out in the context of the unique supranational legislative, judicial, and administrative structure of the European Community.[19] Even within the European Union, however, important nondiscriminatory structural barriers to trade in financial services among the member states are still in place (see chapter 5).

The GATS addresses certain types of second-pillar barriers. Article III (Transparency) imposes a general transparency obligation on WTO members to publish all measures "of general application" that are relevant to trade in services.[20] Article VI (Domestic Regulation) addresses, in fairly general terms, barriers created by domestic regulations. It requires countries to apply such regulations in a "reasonable, objective and impartial manner" to avoid undermining commitments to market access and national treatment.[21] Moreover, countries must have appropriate legal procedures to review administrative decisions affecting trade in services.[22] Article VI also mandates further work to develop disciplines to ensure that licensing requirements or technical standards do not constitute unnecessary barriers to trade in services. Pending the completion of this work, countries must refrain from adopting licensing rules or technical standards that are so burdensome, restrictive of trade, or lacking in transparency that they undermine the benefits that could reasonably be expected from their commitments to national treatment and market access.[23]

The GATS deals with additional second-pillar barriers for individual sectors in members' schedules of commitments. The most far-reaching example is in basic telecommunications, where a substantial majority of the countries that have made commitments to national treatment and market access in that sector have incorporated into their schedules— using the "additional commitments" column—a reference paper setting forth "procompetitive" regulatory principles.[24] Designed for a sector where dominant suppliers often control essential host-country facilities, these principles seek to ensure that a country's national treatment and market access commitments will not be undermined. Countries committing to the principles undertake, among other things, to maintain measures to ensure network interconnection on nondiscriminatory terms and to prevent certain anticompetitive practices.[25]

In the financial services sector, most OECD countries addressed nondiscriminatory structural barriers in their 1997 schedules of commitments simply by making a general "best efforts" commitment to remove or eliminate any significant adverse effects of such barriers.[26] In addition, the United States and the European Union used the additional commitments column of their schedules to make "best efforts" commitments to remove specified nondiscriminatory barriers. For example, the U.S. administration committed to try to work with the Congress to remove Glass-Steagall Act restrictions, a goal that was subsequently accomplished, while the European Union pledged that its member states would try to process applications for licenses for banking and insurance subsidiaries within specified periods of time. Japan, under great pressure from its trading partners, went further and made binding commitments regarding removal of certain second-pillar barriers—including restrictions on asset-management services and lack of regulatory transparency and limitations on lines of business in insurance—that were covered in its bilateral financial services agreements with the United States (see chapters 4 and 5).

Freedom of Capital Movements. The third pillar of liberalization involves achieving freedom of capital movements across national borders. Such movements comprise international capital transactions—that is, the creation, transfer of ownership, or liquidation of capital assets, including financial assets—and the payments and transfers associated with such transactions.[27] Restrictions on international capital movements are usually imposed on the underlying transactions as opposed to the related payments and transfers.[28] For example, if a country wished to restrict foreign direct investment in the banking sector, it could prohibit foreign financial firms from acquiring significant ownership interests in host-country banks: it would be unusual to try to achieve this result by permitting the acquisition of the ownership interests while using exchange controls to block payment for them.[29]

Although the free movement of capital plays a critical role in allowing efficient allocation of resources on a global basis, the Asian financial crisis of 1997–98 revived a long-standing debate over the appropriateness and effectiveness of capital controls, particularly on short-term flows.[30] Nevertheless, all parties to the debate agree that capital controls can never be a substitute for sound macroeconomic policies and fundamental reforms of domestic financial and legal structures. Indeed, the Asian crisis itself emphasized that weaknesses in domestic financial systems can create significant vulnerabilities as capital movements are liberalized. At present, conventional wisdom holds that, although imposition of new capital controls should, in general, be avoided, the imposition of limited, temporary capital controls to deal with massive temporary inflows or outflows of short-term debt might be useful in some cases.[31] Moreover, it is now widely recognized that removal of existing controls must be carried out with great care. Of particular importance are the pace and appropriate "sequencing" of liberalization of different types of capital flows and of liberalization of capital movements vis-à-vis structural reforms to strengthen domestic financial systems.[32]

Freedom of capital movements per se is not within the purview of the GATS; international capital movements and international trade in financial services are, however, closely related. Establishment of a commercial presence in a host country by a foreign service supplier involves both trade in services under the GATS and international capital transactions. For example, a commitment in the GATS to liberalize financial services trade by allowing foreign financial firms to establish wholly owned subsidiaries is essentially a commitment to allow foreign direct investment that involves the acquisition of 100 percent of the shares of existing or *de novo* host-country financial firms.[33] In theory it is possible that, once established, the subsidiary could conduct its ongoing activities without engaging in additional international capital transactions; however, its activities would need to be limited to transactions with host-country residents involving domestic financial assets.[34]

Establishment and operation of branches, which are not separately incorporated in the host country, virtually always involve international capital transactions between the bank's head office and the branch.[35] These transactions include both foreign direct investment and portfolio investment.[36] For branches conducting a wholesale business, ongoing activities would typically also involve international capital transactions with unaffiliated parties.

For cross-border financial services, international capital transactions are typically either integral to, or closely associated with, the provision of the service. For example, international capital transactions are an integral part of accepting deposits from or making loans to nonresidents. In addition, international capital transactions are usually, although not necessarily, associated with financial services such as securities trading or asset management on behalf of a customer residing in another country.[37] By contrast, certain cross-border financial services, such as investment advisory services and financial information services, can be provided without an associated international capital transaction. The usefulness of investment advice might be limited, however, if the customer were prohibited from investing in foreign assets.

In general, it is difficult to realize fully the benefits of liberalization of trade in financial services without freedom of capital movements. Financial services trade absolutely requires, however, the liberalization of only those capital movements that are necessary for the trade transaction to occur. In recognition of this relationship, Article XI of the GATS (Payments and Transfers) prohibits WTO members from imposing restrictions on capital transactions or associated payments and transfers that would be inconsistent with their specific commitments to liberalization of trade in services.[38] A footnote to Article XVI (Market Access) provides greater detail—namely, a country that has made a specific commitment to market access must allow (a) capital movements that are "essential" for the provision of a service in mode 1 (cross-border supply); and (b) inward capital movements that are "related" to a service supplied through establishment of a commercial presence.[39]

The bottom line is that if a country makes a commitment to liberalize trade with respect to a particular financial service in the GATS, it is also making a commitment to liberalize most capital movements associated with the trade liberalization commitment. The country is not, however, making an across-the-board commitment to freedom of capital movements. The GATS provisions dealing with capital movements, like GATS specific commitments to liberalize trade in services, are subject to a balance-of-payments safeguard.[40] Both the capital movements and balance-of-payments safeguard provisions of the GATS refer to and are consistent with the IMF's responsibilities in these areas.[41]

Strengthening Domestic Financial Systems

The financial services sector has an elaborate and intensively used framework of international fora that are used, both separately and in combination,

to address overall financial and regulatory policy issues; to promote cooperation and coordination among supervisors; to set voluntary but widely
accepted international minimum standards and codes of good practices;
and, most recently, to provide "surveillance" of domestic financial systems.
This surveillance includes monitoring and helping to build institutional
capacity for implementation of the international standards and codes.
The international fora dealing with these issues include the Group of Seven
(G-7), the Group of Ten (G-10), the Group of Twenty (G-20), the Financial
Stability Forum, the Basel Committee on Banking Supervision (Basel
Committee), and the International Organization of Securities Commissions
(IOSCO), as well as the IMF and the World Bank.[42]

The international framework for the financial services sector, which
has been constructed over the past quarter century and is still evolving, is
a response to two major factors: the internationalization of banking and
other financial activities; and the special characteristics of the financial
sector, especially the phenomenon of "systemic risk." Because of systemic
risk, problems with one financial firm can be transmitted to unrelated
financial firms, both within and beyond a single country. For example, a
chain reaction of problems could be triggered through imitative runs on
banks as depositors lose confidence in a banking system, through default
on domestic or international interbank obligations, or through domestic
or international payment systems. Problems in a country's financial sector
can also affect the real economy, both domestically and internationally,
through declines in output and shifts in trade flows.

In addition, the existence of global financial firms, with activities
falling within many different national jurisdictions, requires cooperation
and coordination among home- and host-country authorities to prevent
gaps in supervision. Increasingly, these global firms are financial conglomerates, which means that supervisory cooperation and coordination
are necessary across financial subsectors as well as national borders.

For these reasons, countries have a stake in the quality of each
other's regulation and supervision of the financial sector and also in ensuring cooperation and coordination among supervisors. In this regard it is
useful to distinguish between prudential *regulation*, which includes, for
example, capital and other requirements designed to ensure the safety and

soundness of financial institutions, and *supervision*, which is aimed at making certain that financial firms adhere to such requirements. The importance of strong, effective supervision cannot be overemphasized; without it, the best prudential rules can be meaningless in practice. The extent to which both experience and good judgment are required for such supervision also needs to be emphasized. Indeed, the role and nature of supervision make it particularly difficult for supervisory authorities to reach recognition agreements based on the harmonization of prudential rules (see chapter 5).

While regulation and supervision must be strong and effective, a further complication is that a poorly designed regulatory system—for example, an excessively generous deposit-insurance scheme—can create an unacceptable degree of moral hazard; that is, it may encourage excessive risk-taking by regulated firms. Accordingly, national regulatory and supervisory systems must be designed to complement and support, but not to substitute for, market discipline. Thus, achieving widespread transparency in both the public and private sectors, including accurate and timely disclosure of financial information, is critical for strong financial systems.

Minimum Standards and Codes of Good Practices. Over time, the scope of the international work has expanded from regulation and supervision of internationally active banks to the strength of entire domestic financial systems.[43] International minimum standards and codes of good practices have been established in three broad areas that are of fundamental importance for sound financial systems: (1) transparency of macroeconomic policy and data; (2) institutional and market infrastructure, which includes insolvency, corporate governance, accounting, auditing, market integrity and functioning, and payment and settlement systems; and (3) prudential regulation and supervision, which covers both financial firms and regulatory and supervisory systems.[44]

Although widely accepted, the international minimum standards and codes of good practices are *not* binding agreements in international law. Instead, the standards and codes are developed in the various international fora dealing with financial systems, and market and peer pressures are extremely important in their acceptance throughout the world. In the banking sector, for example, in 1997 the Basel Committee published the Core Principles for Effective Banking Supervision (Basel Core Principles), which it had developed in collaboration with supervisory authorities from fifteen emerging market economies.[45] Subsequently, these principles were widely endorsed by supervisory authorities from both industrial and emerging market economies. Similarly, in the securities sector, IOSCO developed the Objectives and Principles of Securities Regulation, which were endorsed by its worldwide membership in 1998.[46]

"Surveillance." The IMF and the World Bank are playing a major role in fostering implementation of the minimum standards and codes of good practices, including those established for national regulatory and supervisory systems by specialized fora such as the Basel Committee. The IMF's intensive involvement in financial infrastructure issues, which goes well beyond its traditional focus on macroeconomic policy measures, began in the 1990s in country-assistance programs for transition economies of Central and Eastern Europe and the former Soviet Union. During the 1997–98 Asian financial crisis, the conditionality in IMF programs gave new prominence to measures to restructure and strengthen the financial sector, including prudential regulation and supervision.[47] In 1999, the IMF decided to place greater emphasis on financial systems in its routine surveillance of economic developments and policies in its member countries (so-called Article IV surveillance). The World Bank and the regional multilateral development banks have also been placing new emphasis on the strength of countries' financial sectors.

The IMF and the World Bank are coordinating their financial sector surveillance efforts under a joint Financial Sector Assessment Program (FSAP), which they have characterized as a "comprehensive health check-up of a country's financial sector."[48] This includes identifying the strengths and vulnerabilities of a country's financial system; determining whether effective risk-management techniques are being used; and evaluating the observance of internationally accepted standards and codes.[49] For countries that are seeking to build institutional capacity and remedy any deficiencies identified in the assessment, the IMF and the World Bank have committed to ensure that appropriate technical assistance is available.[50]

In designing and carrying out the assessments, the international financial institutions are relying heavily on the work of specialized, sector-specific fora and on national supervisory authorities. For example, a subgroup of the Basel Committee has developed detailed criteria that the IMF and the World Bank are using to assess compliance with the Basel Core Principles, and the country-assessment teams include national supervisors.[51] Besides the need for senior-level supervisory expertise, challenges for the FSAP include establishing a more systematic mechanism for follow-up surveillance and technical assistance in problem areas, and ensuring consistency of assessments across countries. In any case, the IMF and World Bank assessments are not meant to substitute for host-country evaluation of the adequacy of home-country supervision of an individual applicant, market evaluations of the strength of financial firms or systems, or a country's self-evaluation of its regulatory and supervisory system.[52]

The Prudential Carve-Out in the GATS

Notwithstanding the scope and intensity of international efforts to strengthen domestic financial systems, the ultimate responsibility for regulating and supervising banks and other financial firms lies with national authorities.[53] Moreover, the internationally established prudential standards for financial firms are minimum standards; they do not constitute either ceilings (maximum standards) or full harmonization (uniform standards). Thus host-country regulatory authorities may, in accordance with national law, apply prudential rules that are more stringent than the international standards. Moreover, even if both host- and home-country regulators use the international minimum standards, the host-country authorities are not required to rely on a home-country's determination that a particular foreign firm has, in fact, met those standards.

The GATS Annex on Financial Services contains a so-called prudential carve-out for domestic regulation of financial services. This provision, which was included at the insistence of financial regulators, allows a WTO member to take prudential measures "for the protection of investors, depositors, policy holders or persons to whom a fiduciary duty is owed" or "to ensure the integrity and stability of the financial system" regardless of any other provisions of the GATS.[54] Thus prudential measures could, in principle, be inconsistent with a country's national treatment or market access commitments or its MFN obligation. To guard against abuse of the prudential carve-out, the GATS provides that prudential measures may not be used as a means of avoiding a country's obligations or commitments under the agreement.

In one very important respect, the prudential carve-out in the GATS differs from other domestic policy exceptions contained in that agreement.[55] In contrast to health and safety, for example, where only "necessary" measures are excepted, *all* prudential measures are excepted.[56] As a result, a prudential measure may not be challenged on the grounds of whether it is "necessary" or "least trade restrictive." Moreover, the prudential carve-out overrides the requirements for domestic regulations in Article VI of the GATS, discussed earlier.

The absence of a necessity test does not, however, resolve the issue of whether a measure is prudential or is being used to avoid the obligations of the agreement. An allegedly prudential measure that violates a country's obligations or commitments under the GATS might be challenged on the grounds that its real purpose is trade restrictive rather than prudential and therefore it does not fall within the scope of the prudential carve-out. This question is subject to WTO dispute settlement procedures and potentially to a determination by a dispute settlement panel.[57]

Financial regulators do not seem particularly concerned about this possibility. For one thing, prudential issues are dealt with intensively in other international fora, so there is some basis for assuming that certain types of rules will always be considered prudential. Moreover, a WTO member that was concerned about whether a particular measure would be generally accepted as prudential had the option of listing that measure as a limitation when making commitments for national treatment and market access. Another extremely important reason for the apparent lack of concern is that only governments, not private parties, may bring claims to dispute settlement in the WTO. Absent a truly egregious action, governments may prefer to respect each other's ability to determine which rules may be prudential.[58] If a prudential or other financial services issue did reach a WTO dispute settlement panel, the panel would be required, in accordance with the GATS Annex on Financial Services, to have the expertise necessary to deal with "the specific financial service under dispute"—a provision that finance officials had insisted on.[59]

4

National Treatment and Market Access

—⟨∾∾⟩—

The negotiations leading to the December 1997 agreement on commitments on financial services focused primarily on first-pillar barriers, that is, barriers to national treatment and market access. Most of the participating countries "bound" the levels of liberalization for foreign direct investment that existed as the negotiations entered their final phase in late 1997. For a number of emerging market economies and other developing countries, such liberalization represented a substantial improvement over the liberalization that existed a few years earlier. Moreover, as noted in chapter 1, capturing existing levels of liberalization in binding commitments subject to WTO dispute settlement is important in its own right. In contrast to the commitments for foreign direct investment, the 1997 commitments for cross-border services in mode 1 (cross-border supply) were, even for OECD countries, relatively limited and did not always reflect existing liberalization.

The results of the 1997 negotiations—that is, the financial services schedules of commitments and lists of MFN exemptions—were incorporated into the GATS by the Fifth Protocol to the GATS, which entered into force on March 1, 1999.[1] Seventy-one WTO members made improved—or, in a few cases, first-time—financial services commitments, although the strength and scope of these commitments vary substantially.[2] However, as of January 2003, the commitments made by six of the participating countries had not entered into force because these countries had not yet accepted the Fifth Protocol.[3]

Financial services commitments have been made by additional WTO members that were not parties to the 1997 agreement. As of January 2003, fourteen countries that became members of the WTO under standard accession procedures after its establishment in 1995 and did not participate in the 1997 negotiations had made commitments in financial services.[4] These acceding countries have, in general, made strong financial services commitments, including new liberalization, for foreign direct investment and, in many cases, cross-border services. Twenty-nine other WTO members—mainly small developing countries— that did not participate in the 1997 negotiations maintained their pre-existing financial services schedules, which, in general, include only minimal commitments.[5] One additional member made a first-time commitment in financial services in 1998.[6]

When all of these commitments are taken into account, the number of countries that have taken on commitments in financial services in the GATS is substantial.[7] As of January 1, 2003, 115 members of the WTO— 80 percent of its total membership of 144—had made commitments in financial services including insurance.[8] These numbers do not, of course, provide any indication of the strength or scope of commitments.

Indeed, significant gaps remain in the GATS commitments to national treatment and market access for financial services. These include both (a) "binding gaps," which are created by the failure to bind in the GATS liberalizing measures already in effect or scheduled to go into effect; and (b) gaps resulting from barriers that countries continue to impose on foreign financial services and service suppliers. This chapter examines the gaps in the GATS financial services commitments, beginning with an overview of the issues involved in binding existing or ongoing liberalization. It then examines, in turn, the gaps in the commitments for services provided through establishment of a commercial presence (mode 3) and services provided across borders (modes 1 and 2). The chapter highlights the types of barriers that have posed ongoing problems, but it does not provide a guide to the specific barriers that individual countries impose.[9]

"Binding" Existing and Ongoing Liberalization

Eliminating binding gaps by capturing existing and ongoing liberalization as formal GATS commitments is an important goal for the Doha round financial services negotiations.[10] A last-minute cliffhanger issue in negotiating the December 1997 agreement on financial services commitments—

namely, whether Japan would bind in the GATS the measures it had agreed to in bilateral financial services agreements with the United States—highlights the significance of binding such liberalization. In accordance with the GATS, these measures were already being applied to all WTO members on an MFN basis. Nevertheless, the United States and other WTO members considered it essential for Japan to include the measures in its GATS schedule of commitments so that they would become formal multilateral commitments directly and fully subject to WTO dispute settlement. In the end, Japan agreed to do so.[11]

In the negotiations leading to the 1997 agreement, some developing countries were reluctant to bind liberalizing measures already in effect, let alone plans for future liberalization. Consider, for example, a host country that allows foreign banks to have 100 percent ownership positions in domestic financial firms. If its GATS schedule of commitments guarantees a foreign ownership interest of, say, only 49 percent, the country has left open the possibility of restricting foreign ownership positions to that level in the future. Indeed, in the 1997 agreement, some emerging market economies scheduled commitments that were more restrictive than measures already in force.

Suppose that the host country in this example enacted a new measure limiting permissible ownership interests for foreign banks to 49 percent, which would be consistent with the commitment it had made in the GATS. Suppose also that the new law applied to foreign banks already in the market, that is, it required them to divest any existing ownership interest in excess of 49 percent of the shares of a domestic financial firm. The measure would still be consistent with the GATS—unless the country had made a commitment, as some WTO members did for financial services, to "grandfather" existing operations and activities. Although grandfathering (also referred to as guaranteeing the retention of "acquired rights") is an important principle that is often used as a basis for national policies dealing with foreign direct investment in the financial sector, it can create inequities between firms already in the market and new entrants. It is therefore not a substitute for a ban on new measures that are inconsistent with market access and national treatment (often referred to as a "standstill").[12]

Since the 1997 agreement, further market opening for financial services has taken place in a number of emerging market economies, either through unilateral action or as part of the conditionality in IMF stabilization programs. Without concomitant changes in GATS commitments, new binding gaps are created. Unlike the financial services chapter of the NAFTA, the GATS does not contain a "ratchet" that would automatically lock in or bind new liberalizing measures that reduce or eliminate barriers to national treatment or market access.[13] Moreover, countries that have adopted liberalizing measures are concerned about receiving "credit" for such measures in the Doha round.[14] This concern highlights a major "disconnect" between trade negotiations and economic theory—namely, trade negotiations involve exchanging so-called concessions of liberalization that, in economic terms, are in a country's best interest in the first place.

IMF Conditionality. The IMF may not impose so-called cross-conditionality in its stabilization programs that would directly subject the disbursement of IMF loans to the rules or decisions of other international organizations.[15] Thus, although IMF conditionality could overlap with measures a country has undertaken as GATS commitments, the IMF could not require a country to fulfill its GATS commitments per se. Similarly, the IMF could not require a borrowing country to transform liberalizing measures undertaken as part of the conditionality in an IMF program into binding commitments in the GATS.[16] During the Asian financial crisis, however, an undertaking involving GATS commitments was included in the economic program that Korea submitted to the IMF in February 1998.[17]

In its negotiations with the IMF, Korea had agreed to include a wide-ranging set of structural measures in its economic program in an effort to restore confidence and signal to the markets that it was indeed undertaking major policy reform.[18] Among the measures Korea listed was strengthening its GATS financial services commitments to correspond to the liberalization commitments it had made as part of its accession to the OECD in 1996. The issue arose largely because Korea's refusal in the 1997 financial services negotiations to bind the liberalizing measures it had undertaken for its OECD accession had created visible and contentious binding gaps in its GATS commitments. Although Korea upgraded its GATS schedule of commitments in early 1999, binding gaps still remain; the reason is that Korea used its OECD commitments as the basis for upgrading its GATS schedule, as opposed to the stronger and more rapid liberalization it undertook in connection with its IMF program.[19]

Permanence of GATS Commitments. A major reason for the existence of binding gaps is that GATS commitments are subject to enforcement through the WTO dispute settlement mechanism and may not be withdrawn without compensation of trading partners. The GATS does, however, provide a balance-of-payments safeguard that allows commitments to be suspended temporarily in the event of "serious balance-of-payments and external financial difficulties or threat thereof," subject to certain conditions.[20]

The Uruguay Round negotiations reached no agreement on the issue of a more general "emergency" safeguard that some envisaged as a GATS counterpart to the GATT safeguard provision dealing with an unforeseen import surge that causes or threatens serious injury to domestic producers. The deadline for agreement has been extended several times, most recently to March 2004, and a number of members have circulated discussion papers. No consensus has emerged, however, on the need for—or terms of—an emergency safeguard provision in the GATS, primarily because the issues are more complicated for services than for goods. For one thing, the GATS includes services provided through establishment of a commercial presence; for another, the issues vary among services sectors.[21]

Article XXI of the GATS (Modification of Schedules) provides a mechanism for permanent modification of commitments, but, as of January 2003, it had not yet been tested. Under Article XXI, once three years have elapsed from the entry into force of its specific commitments, a country may modify its schedule of commitments if compensatory adjustment is provided to its trading partners. WTO members did not agree on the procedures under which such a modification may be carried out until 1999.[22] Moreover, for the regulatory and quantitative barriers at issue for financial and other services, it is not clear how these procedures will work in practice.[23]

In the case of tariffs on goods, changing a commitment and providing compensatory adjustment are relatively easy. A country that was unable to meet its commitment to reduce tariffs on rubber footwear, for example, could provide compensation by lowering its tariff on, say, corned beef. By contrast, if foreign direct investment is involved, retracting a commitment might be associated with a divestiture requirement. Even without divestiture, retracting a commitment regarding foreign ownership positions could have the effect of discriminating between new foreign entrants to the market and foreign firms with existing operations.[24]

If a country does not invoke Article XXI and simply fails to honor a commitment, its trading partners may resort to the WTO dispute settlement mechanism. This process begins with consultations, and, if the matter remains unresolved, provides for a dispute settlement panel, the option of appealing a panel decision to a standing Appellate Body, and ultimately the possibility of WTO-sanctioned retaliatory measures. Such sanctions are supposed to be a temporary remedy until the offending country has complied with the decision, but, in some cases, sanctions have been in effect for considerable periods of time. No supranational mechanism exists to enforce the rulings of a dispute settlement panel. Consequently, "moral suasion" plays an important role, along with the economic cost associated with sanctions and the international political cost of failing to comply.[25]

Foreign Direct Investment

Ideally, WTO members would make broad commitments covering all types of financial services for the establishment and expansion of a commercial presence in whatever legal form the investor chooses. Indeed, most OECD countries used the Understanding on Commitments in Financial Services to make such commitments.[26] A number of additional WTO members, including most acceding countries, made similar commitments. Other members, however, have significant gaps in their financial services commitments for establishment of a commercial presence. Although some of these gaps represent binding gaps, such as the binding of foreign ownership positions at less than levels currently permitted, many represent barriers that members continue to impose. Dealing with these remaining barriers is another major goal for the Doha round financial services negotiations and involves two elements: first, convincing a country to change its national laws or regulations to remove the barriers; and second, convincing the country to bind the associated liberalization in the GATS.[27]

Remaining Barriers to Entry and Operation. Despite significant improvements during the course of the Uruguay Round, some WTO members still impose major barriers to entry for foreign financial firms. Restrictions on foreign ownership positions in a number of emerging market economies and other developing countries prevent foreign financial firms from holding majority-ownership positions in host-country firms, or, where majority ownership is allowed, limit the ownership position to less than 100 percent. Another major barrier involves restricting the type of legal entity through which financial services may be provided by prohibiting entry through the branch form of organization—that is, through direct branches of a foreign financial firm.

Other important discriminatory barriers relate to the operation of foreign financial firms once they have established a commercial presence in the host country. For banking services, these barriers include limitations on the number of branches that a subsidiary of a foreign bank may open, the number of ATM machines it may install, and the types of banking services it may offer to domestic residents. Discriminatory barriers to host-country operations faced by firms engaging in securities activities often include restrictions on their participation in underwriting and distributing securities and their ability to trade securities in secondary markets.[28] Foreign financial firms may also face discriminatory barriers arising from limitations on the temporary entry of home-country personnel for employment by their subsidiaries or branches.[29]

An additional problem arises when a host country has adopted and bound liberalizing measures for only one type of financial service and has failed to include, or has placed severe limitations on, other important financial services subsectors or activities. For example, a number of countries, particularly emerging market economies and other developing countries, have made stronger and broader commitments for banking services than for securities-related services. Furthermore, many countries did not make commitments for asset management or financial information services. As financial service providers engage in an increasingly broad range of activities in their home countries that cut across financial subsectors, they may find such disparities in host-country liberalization increasingly burdensome.

MFN Exemptions. Although exemptions from the MFN obligation of the GATS are logically distinct from national treatment and market access barriers, they are closely related. An MFN exemption allows a country to apply more favorable treatment than that guaranteed by its GATS commitments on a non-MFN basis, but it does not permit less favorable treatment. As a result, an MFN exemption, combined with the absence of commitments to substantially full national treatment and market access, provides leeway for a country to pursue a unilateral reciprocity policy.[30] Such policies constitute a significant departure from the fundamental principle of nondiscrimination among countries on which the GATS and other multilateral trade agreements are based. The GATS nonetheless allows one-time MFN exemptions to be taken upon entry into force of a country's initial schedule of commitments under the GATS.[31] In principle such MFN exemptions should not exceed a period of ten years; they must be reviewed after five years and, in any event, are subject to negotiation in subsequent trade-liberalizing rounds.

In financial services, about twenty-five WTO members have taken Article II (MFN) exemptions.[32] Many of these exemptions are relatively narrow, that is, they apply only to a specific activity or to treatment accorded particular countries. The United States, for example, has taken an MFN exemption for granting primary dealer status to foreign financial firms operating in the U.S. government securities market.[33] Some members, including a number of developing countries, have taken MFN exemptions for measures applicable to neighboring countries because of special relationships that do not qualify as economic integration agreements.[34]

Of the members with MFN exemptions in financial services, about half have taken broad exemptions covering establishment of subsidiaries and/or branches of foreign financial firms—that is, they enable the country to condition establishment on whether the firm's home country has opened its market to host-country financial firms. These broad MFN exemptions—and concomitant absence of commitments or only minimal commitments to market access and national treatment—have been taken either to accommodate reciprocity policies currently in force or to preserve the option of applying such policies in the future. In the latter case, the MFN exemption is analogous to a binding gap.

In either case, a goal for the financial services negotiations is the narrowing or withdrawal of broad MFN exemptions to reduce or eliminate the scope for unilateral reciprocity policies. Ideally, removal of a broad MFN exemption should be accompanied by stronger underlying commitments to market access and national treatment. If a country strengthens its commitments but does not withdraw its broad MFN exemption, the scope for unilateral reciprocity policies is reduced but not eliminated.

Barriers within the Scope of the Prudential Carve-Out. Treatment of direct branches of foreign banks illustrates not only the importance of providing market access and national treatment but also the difficulties of dealing with barriers that may fall within the prudential carve-out. Barriers to market access listed in Article XVI of the GATS (Market Access) include restrictions on the type of legal entity through which services may be supplied; this reflects a consensus that an overall prohibition on branch entry is not a legitimate prudential measure. If branch entry is permitted, even though the branch is an integral part of the foreign bank and not separately capitalized, countries sometimes impose branch capital-equivalency requirements. These can take the form of "dotation" or endowment capital requirements or asset pledge requirements.[35] Because such measures are widely regarded as prudential, most countries that impose these requirements have not listed them as limitations on market access or national treatment in their schedules of commitments.[36]

Some host countries take a further step that effectively negates the economic benefits associated with the branch form of organization—namely, calculating lending and other operating limits based on branch capital-equivalency requirements. Such measures restrict branch operations by, for example, tying the size of individual loans to the amount of capital attributable to the branch. Since domestic banks operate on the basis of their consolidated worldwide capital, national treatment would require allowing branches to operate on the basis of the foreign bank's consolidated worldwide capital. A U.S. government study concluded that although restrictions might need to be applied to address specific prudential concerns in problem cases, general application of such restrictions would have the effect of denying a foreign bank the economic benefits of the branch form of organization.[37]

Some countries that impose lending and other operating limits based on branch capital-equivalency requirements—Korea and Turkey, for example—listed the measures as limitations in their schedules of commitments, which could be interpreted as an acknowledgment that these measures may not be generally accepted as prudential.[38] By contrast, countries that impose the measures but did not list them as limitations in their schedules—Chile, for example—clearly believe the measures are within the scope of the prudential carve-out. The EU simply noted that branches (as opposed to subsidiaries) of third-country financial firms are, in general, not subject to harmonized EU prudential measures and that each member state may therefore impose its own measures for prudential purposes.[39]

A measure that imposes lending and other operating limits based on branch capital-equivalency requirements on all host-country branches of foreign banks arguably does not meet a "necessary" or "least trade restrictive" test. Prudential measures, however, are not subject to such tests (see chapter 3). The measure could nonetheless be challenged, at least in theory, under the antiabuse provision of the prudential carve-out on the grounds that it was being used to avoid a country's commitment to allow entry through the branch form of organization. In practice, however, it seems highly unlikely that national authorities would use the WTO dispute settlement mechanism, as opposed to a more informal forum, to challenge such a measure.

What then are the options for dealing with these kinds of barriers? One approach would have home-country financial regulatory authorities convince host-country authorities that their prudential concerns can be addressed without imposing such requirements across the board. These efforts could take place bilaterally, or in various international fora, including the financial services negotiations held under the auspices of the WTO, where finance ministries play a major role.[40] If a country had relied on the prudential carve-out, however, eliminating the measure would not require a change in its schedule of commitments in the GATS, because the measure would not have been listed in the first place.

A second approach would have home- and host-country authorities negotiate a recognition arrangement. An example of such an arrangement is Germany's recognition of U.S. supervision to provide relief from the lending and other operational limits based on dotation capital requirements that Germany imposes on branches of non-EU banks.[41] Under authority granted by the German Banking Act, German regulatory authorities have "recognized" U.S. regulation and supervision, together with assurances of enhanced supervisory cooperation, as sufficient to exempt branches of U.S. banks from these restrictions. Accordingly, these branches are now subject to limits that are based on the consolidated worldwide capital of the U.S. bank rather than on dotation capital requirements.

This result was achieved through negotiations and an exchange of letters between U.S. and German supervisory authorities and was implemented by a regulation issued by the German finance ministry in 1994.[42] Although the GATS is permissive with regard to such recognition arrangements, the WTO would not be the appropriate forum for negotiating them. The provision of the GATS regarding recognition of prudential measures is discussed in detail in the following chapter on nondiscriminatory structural barriers because most prudential measures, unlike branch operating limits based on capital-equivalency requirements, are consistent with national treatment and market access.

Cross-Border Services

Because of the difficulty of making meaningful distinctions between financial services provided in mode 1 (cross-border supply) and those provided in mode 2 (consumption abroad), the term "cross-border services" is used broadly in this study to cover both modes (see chapter 2). Financial services commitments in the GATS differ substantially, however, both between the two modes and among countries. Most OECD countries used the Understanding on Commitments in Financial Services to make broad commitments in mode 2 but to make commitments in mode 1 for only two categories of financial services: (a) financial information and data processing services; and (b) advisory services.[43] Many of the acceding countries have made substantial commitments in mode 1 as well as mode 2.[44] Most developing countries, however, made no commitments or extremely limited commitments for cross-border financial services.

Binding Gaps versus Remaining Barriers. For a number of the OECD countries, the lack of broad cross-border commitments in mode 1 (cross-border supply) constitutes a binding gap. These countries have been unwilling to bind additional categories of services even when their existing rules are consistent with market access and national treatment under the GATS. Some OECD countries, however, restrict or prohibit the cross-border provision of financial services, particularly securities services—for example, by requiring establishment of a commercial presence to provide securities services to retail customers. In some cases, host countries may regard these barriers as prudential.[45]

Although the lack of broad cross-border commitments by some emerging market economies or other developing countries also represents a binding gap, many developing countries continue to impose barriers that significantly restrict or prohibit the provision of cross-border financial services to their residents.[46] Cross-border trade in financial services can benefit host-country consumers and contribute to the development of more competitive host-country markets. From the perspective of developing countries, however, cross-border services may not appear to offer the same benefits as establishment of a commercial presence, particularly the transfer of technology, know-how, and skills. A further complication is that capital flows are either an integral part of, or typically associated with, most types of cross-border financial services (see chapter 3). In addition to their concern about the overall volatility of international capital flows, some developing countries may be concerned about "capital flight" on the part of individual residents.[47] Restrictions on residents' opening bank accounts abroad, for example, constitute both capital controls and barriers to trade in financial services.

Developing countries should be encouraged to liberalize trade in cross-border services, but they can reasonably be asked to bind in the GATS only what OECD countries are willing to bind. In the 1997 agreement, the failure of a number of OECD countries to make broad cross-border financial services commitments in mode 1 that fully encompassed existing levels of liberalization appears to have been associated with several factors. These include uncertainty about WTO jurisprudence, more liberal regulatory treatment that goes beyond national treatment for some wholesale cross-border services, and ongoing work on regulatory responses to the potential use of the Internet for retail cross-border financial services. In setting priorities for the negotiations on financial services in the Doha round, it is important to recognize that the first two factors remain unchanged and that, despite progress with regard to e-finance regulatory issues since 1997, the third factor also remains important.

Uncertainty about WTO Jurisprudence. An important reason for the OECD countries' reluctance to make cross-border commitments is that financial regulatory authorities are uncertain about potential interpretations of GATS commitments in an area that is extremely complex. Because the WTO dispute settlement system is as yet untested for financial services in general—and for cross-border financial services in particular—no body of established WTO jurisprudence exists in this area.

A related consideration involves the prudential carve-out. Even if a host country's prudential rules governing cross-border financial services were found to be inconsistent with a binding commitment to national treatment and market access, those rules would presumably fall within the prudential carve-out. Countries may be reluctant, however, to make commitments to national treatment and market access for cross-border services that have the potential to overburden the prudential carve-out. Moreover, the scope of the carve-out, particularly its antiabuse provision, is still untested in WTO jurisprudence.

More Liberal Approaches for Wholesale Services. For financial services provided across borders to wholesale customers, most OECD countries provide, at a minimum, national treatment and market access. Moreover, even outside the EU single-market program, countries sometimes provide treatment that goes beyond national treatment and into second-pillar liberalization. For example, most OECD countries do not impose a host-country regulatory regime on banking services supplied to wholesale customers. In addition, a number of OECD countries provide certain exceptions from host-country securities regulations for cross-border services provided to wholesale customers, particularly other financial services firms.[48] This approach does not, however, constitute recognition of the adequacy of specific home-country regulatory regimes; instead, it appears to reflect the view that host-country regulation is unnecessary because the customers have the expertise required to conduct their own risk assessments.

Second-pillar liberalization raises the question of whether, or to what extent, liberalizing measures that go beyond national treatment and market access should be bound in the GATS as so-called additional commitments (see chapter 5). With regard to prudential measures, however, it is difficult to imagine that regulatory authorities would be willing to bind in the GATS measures granting certain exemptions from prudential rules that provide national treatment and market access in the first place. If such measures were bound as additional commitments, host-country regulatory authorities would presumably need to rely on the GATS prudential carve-out should the need arise to reimpose the rules on a national treatment basis. Moreover, the uncertainty about WTO jurisprudence that was a factor in the unwillingness of OECD countries to make broad commitments to market access and national treatment in mode 1 would presumably be even more important with regard to binding an exemption from a prudential measure.

Evolving Regulatory Responses to Retail Cross-Border Services. At the time of the 1997 negotiations, financial regulatory authorities were in the early stages of examining the applicability of their existing regulatory frameworks to financial services provided through the Internet. For this reason as well, countries were unwilling to make binding commitments in a multilateral trade agreement subject to dispute settlement. This reluctance applied even in the case of binding gaps, that is, when countries provided—and planned to continue to provide—national treatment for cross-border services.

Host countries that allow retail cross-border financial services usually require foreign service providers to meet host-country licensing or registration requirements on a national treatment basis. Foreign financial firms, however, may find it extremely difficult to meet the high regulatory standards for licensing or registration applicable to host-country financial firms, without establishing a commercial presence in the host country. Such barriers, in general, constitute second-pillar barriers because they arise from nondiscriminatory national rules.

Beginning in the late 1990s, a number of national regulatory authorities clarified the circumstances under which they would exercise authority over cross-border securities activities, especially activities conducted via the Internet.[49] The criteria that have generally been used, which were set forth in a 1998 IOSCO recommendation, make it possible for foreign service providers—despite the global reach of the Internet—to take steps to insulate their web sites from potential host-country customers to avoid triggering host-country licensing or registration requirements.[50]

A country's decision to refrain from exercising regulatory authority because a foreign financial firm is not dealing with host-country residents should, however, be distinguished from a situation in which the host country does not impose its own rules because it is willing to "recognize" home-country regulation and supervision. Indeed, one issue for future regulation of cross-border retail financial services is the extent to which it may become increasingly difficult to impose host-country rules. Greater reliance on home-country rules would, however, require a major consumer education effort as well as increased cooperation and coordination among regulatory authorities. The issues are much more complex for retail than for wholesale cross-border services because of the strong public policy interest in consumer protection.

Negotiating Goals. The foregoing discussion suggests that, at least in the initial stages of the financial services negotiations in the Doha round, the time may not be ripe for a major breakthrough in obtaining comprehensive cross-border commitments to national treatment and market access in the GATS. The overall goal, of course, needs to be much broader and stronger commitments for services provided across borders through both mode 1 and mode 2. This goal might, however, be most effectively pursued using an incremental approach.

In the Doha round, such an approach might focus on three interim goals:

The first is to broaden the group of countries with mode 1 and 2 commitments that are at least as strong as those made by most OECD countries—that is, advisory services and financial information and data processing services in mode 1 (cross-border supply) and all activities in mode 2 (consumption abroad). Besides these commitments, which are set forth in the Understanding on Commitments in Financial Services, any new commitments that OECD countries are willing to make in the Doha round should be included as part of this effort. For some countries, obtaining commitments commensurate with those made by OECD countries would involve eliminating binding gaps; for others, barriers would need to be lifted and the resulting liberalization bound.

The second interim goal is to explore whether there are any specific categories of financial services, beyond the two now covered by the Understanding on Commitments in Financial Services, that most OECD countries might be willing to bind in mode 1 (cross-border supply). Such an effort could focus on services that are likely to present fewer risks for host-country retail consumers—for example, bank lending (which, in any case, typically represents a binding gap) as opposed to deposit-taking. Such an effort could also focus on the possibility of distinguishing between wholesale and retail customers. For example, countries might be more willing to bind cross-border asset-management services that were provided only to wholesale customers such as pension funds.

The third interim goal for cross-border services involves persuading emerging market and other developing countries that do not currently offer substantially full market access and national treatment for a broad range of activities in mode 1 (cross-border supply) to liberalize their rules.[51] Binding such liberalization in the GATS would necessarily be a goal for future negotiations, since it would not be productive to pressure these countries to make commitments for activities that OECD countries are unwilling to bind.

5

Nondiscriminatory Structural Barriers

—◊◊◊—

A host country's rules may be completely consistent with national treatment and market access in the GATS, but still create nonquantitative and nondiscriminatory structural barriers. The issue for the financial services negotiations in the Doha round is whether, or to what extent, it is realistic or appropriate to negotiate and bind in the GATS second-pillar liberalization—that is, liberalization that goes beyond national treatment and market access.[1] For financial services, second-pillar barriers are often associated with measures taken for prudential purposes. As discussed in chapter 3, such barriers raise two issues: first, the distinction between legitimate prudential measures and measures that are primarily anticompetitive; and second, the scope for reducing barriers created by differences in prudential rules among countries without jeopardizing the underlying purpose of these rules.

This chapter examines three areas of second-pillar liberalization. Two are general GATS issues that are particularly important for the financial services sector. The first is broadening and strengthening disciplines on regulatory transparency—that is, transparency in developing and applying regulations—and the closely related principle of procedural "fairness" in applying regulations. The second involves anticompetitive measures that are consistent with the national treatment and market access articles of the GATS but nonetheless serve primarily to preclude "effective market access" by foreign firms. In the financial sector, such barriers may, at times, inappropriately be justified on prudential grounds.

The third area of second-pillar liberalization examined in this chapter is specific to the financial services sector because it involves measures undertaken for legitimate prudential purposes. This chapter explores further the provision for recognition of prudential measures in the GATS

Annex on Financial Services, which was discussed in chapter 4 in relation to branch lending limits based on dotation capital. The chapter concludes with a discussion of the EU approach to dealing with nondiscriminatory structural barriers in the single-market program for the financial sector and its relevance to international trade in financial services.

Regulatory Transparency

Achieving stronger and broader GATS disciplines to help ensure transparency in domestic regulation is an important goal for the services negotiations in the Doha round.[2] Transparency is widely recognized as a critical element of "good governance" in both the public and private sectors.[3] In the context of the GATS, regulatory transparency and the closely related principle of procedural fairness in applying regulations serve two purposes. First, they could reduce or eliminate nondiscriminatory structural barriers to trade in services created by opaque and unfair regulatory procedures. Second, they could help ensure that a country does not use its regulatory process to undermine its specific commitments to national treatment and market access for foreign services and service suppliers.

Rules about Developing and Applying Rules. Regulatory transparency is qualitatively different from other types of second-pillar liberalization because it involves rules about developing and applying rules, that is, procedural as opposed to substantive barriers. Procedural reform can, however, engender substantive change. Increased transparency in developing and applying regulations, together with procedural fairness in applying regulations, can lead to higher quality regulations. Such regulations are likely to be clearer; more effective and less burdensome in achieving their goals; and applied more reasonably, objectively, and predictably. Regulatory transparency and procedural fairness help to achieve these goals because they promote accountability—that is, they create an environment in which regulatory authorities must explain and accept responsibility for their actions with regard to the development and application of rules.

Transparency in *developing* financial services regulations includes establishing a meaningful procedure for interested parties to comment on a proposed regulation prior to its adoption in final form.[4] Specific approaches will vary among countries—and over time within countries—depending on the legal system, the institutional arrangements for financial regulation and supervision, and the size and stage of development of financial markets. In the United States, for example, the Administrative Procedure Act generally requires "notice and comment" rulemaking, whereby regulatory authorities must give public notice of proposed rules, provide a reasonable amount of time for interested parties to submit comments, give consideration to comments received, and publish final regulations with an explanation that addresses major concerns raised in the comments and gives the basis for the agency's decision.[5]

A basic element of transparency in *applying* financial services regulations is ensuring that service providers are made aware of all statutes, regulations, and administrative decisions relevant to their establishment and operation. Article III of the GATS (Transparency) already requires countries to publish all measures "of general application" relating to trade in services.[6] Other important elements of transparency in applying regulations include establishing and making publicly available objective criteria for obtaining authorization to provide a service; providing information on the amount of time normally required to act upon an application; responding to an applicant's request for information on the status of the application; and, except when special circumstances make it impracticable to do so, providing reasonable advance notice before requiring compliance with new regulations.[7]

Although increased transparency per se should contribute to both substantive and procedural fairness in financial services regulation, principles specifically designed to enhance *procedural fairness in applying* regulations are usually linked with proposals for greater regulatory transparency. Article VI of the GATS (Domestic Regulation) already addresses some basic elements of procedural fairness in applying regulations (see chapter 3). Several of these, however, cover only those services for which specific commitments to national treatment or market access have been made—for example, requirements that regulations must be applied in a "reasonable, objective and impartial manner," and that regulatory authorities must act on applications in a timely fashion.[8] A provision of Article VI that applies more generally requires a country to maintain a mechanism for appeal of an adverse regulatory ruling affecting trade in services.[9]

Independence of the regulator is an essential precondition for procedural fairness—and, indeed, for effective and equitable regulation and supervision in general. As defined by IOSCO, this means that a regulatory agency should be "operationally independent from external political or industry interference in the exercise of its functions and powers."[10] Article VI of the GATS does not address this issue. In the basic telecommunications sector, however, independence of the regulator was included in the reference paper on procompetitive regulatory principles (see chapter 3).

Sound Financial Systems. Strengthening disciplines on regulatory transparency and procedural fairness in the GATS could be designed specifically for individual sectors such as financial services or constructed to apply more generally to all services sectors.[11] In either case, such disciplines would complement the work on transparency that is part of the ongoing international effort to strengthen domestic financial systems. Most of that work focuses on establishing international minimum standards and codes of good practices with regard to other types of transparency: on the part of governments with regard to macroeconomic policy and data; and on the part of the private sector with regard to disclosure of financial information, risk exposure, and risk-management practices.[12]

Some of the international work on transparency related to sound financial systems does, however, deal with regulatory transparency. GATS disciplines on regulatory transparency and procedural fairness could reinforce and build upon the consensus reflected in (a) the IOSCO Objectives and Principles for Securities Regulations, which call for regulators to adopt "clear and consistent regulatory processes"—that is, processes that are "consistently applied, comprehensive, transparent to the public, [and] fair and equitable"[13]—and (b) the IMF Code of Good Practices on Transparency in Monetary and Financial Policies, which includes a presumption in favor of public consultations on proposals for "substantive technical changes" to financial regulations.[14] In addition, GATS disciplines on the independence of financial regulators could reinforce the international work on this principle, which is included in both the IOSCO principles and the Basel Core Principles for Effective Banking Supervision.[15]

Because of the prudential carve-out, financial regulatory authorities may take measures to ensure the integrity and stability of the financial system or to protect consumers of financial services even if these measures are inconsistent with other provisions of the GATS. Nonetheless, it is important that any GATS disciplines on regulatory transparency and procedural fairness—whether they are "horizontal" disciplines that apply to all services or are disciplines specific to financial services—are designed so that financial regulatory authorities can comply without interfering with prudential regulation. Invoking prudential purposes as the basis for either a lack of transparency in developing and applying regulations or a lack of procedural fairness in applying regulations would place an unwarranted burden on the prudential carve-out and defeat the purpose of the disciplines.

"Effective Market Access"

Beyond procedural barriers, an important issue is how far the GATS negotiations and schedules of commitments should proceed into the substance of domestic policy measures that are consistent with Article XVI (Market Access) and Article XVII (National Treatment). In particular, what types of domestic regulatory measures should be scheduled under Article XVIII (Additional Commitments) of the GATS? A useful approach might be to focus on anticompetitive domestic measures that cannot be justified on prudential grounds and serve primarily to keep foreign service suppliers from competing in host-country markets by making entry impractical or too costly—thereby denying them "effective market access."[16]

In the 1997 financial services negotiations, for example, Japan's trading partners regarded certain long-standing domestic policy measures in Japan as serving primarily as barriers to foreign entry that could not be justified on prudential grounds. As a result, these countries pressured Japan to incorporate into its GATS schedule of commitments the measures it had taken to remove such barriers in accordance with bilateral Japan-U.S. agreements (see chapter 4). These measures, for which Japan used the additional commitments column of its GATS schedule, included reducing or eliminating various restrictions on asset-management activities that had the effect of preventing foreign firms from participating in the market. The restrictions included prohibiting a single entity from managing both pension and mutual funds and imposing extremely strict asset-allocation rules—for example, requiring most assets to be invested in bonds and other fixed-income instruments as opposed to equities.[17]

Measures that constitute barriers to effective market access are distinct from the barriers to market access covered by Article XVI of the GATS. The latter constitute quantitative barriers based on criteria such as numerical quotas and economic needs tests that are beyond the control of the affected foreign service supplier to meet.[18] By contrast, measures denying effective market access would, as a legal matter, allow a foreign firm the possibility of complying with the rules—that is, the firm would be permitted to enter the market and operate under the same rules that apply to domestic firms. Even if the rules provided de facto national treatment, however, their practical impact on foreign firms would be to create a major barrier to entry.[19]

In some cases, the original purpose of a measure blocking effective market access to foreign services and service suppliers might have been to keep all new entrants, both domestic and foreign, out of a particular market or market segment. Over time, however, such a measure may have become primarily a barrier to foreign entry, and, in some cases, one that trading partners believe has been deliberately left in place for that reason. Other longstanding anticompetitive measures might originally have been adopted primarily for prudential reasons but can no longer be justified on that basis. Whatever their original purpose, barriers to effective market access could be included in the financial services negotiations in the Doha round with the aim of binding liberalizing measures as "additional commitments" in the GATS.

Identifying barriers to effective market access in financial services that could usefully be negotiated in the Doha round requires a country's trading partners to determine (a) whether, in practice, its measures keep foreign firms from competing in a host-country market or market segment and (b) whether a "critical mass" of regulators believes that the measures are inappropriate for prudential purposes. Even if the prevalent regulatory view is that the measures cannot be justified on prudential grounds, however, host-country regulators must be persuaded to accept it.[20] Some guidance on the areas that are appropriately subject to prudential regulation and the types of measures that are generally accepted as prudential is provided by the international work on minimum standards and codes of good practices. That work does not, however, directly address the appropriateness of specific national measures.

The additional commitments made by Japan in the 1997 agreement on financial services commitments could provide a model for the types of measures that could be negotiated in the Doha round. In particular, a number of countries still maintain substantial restrictions that have the effect of keeping foreign firms from competing in the provision of asset-management services in the host country.[21] One important barrier is created by prohibiting pension and mutual funds from investing in foreign securities or by limiting such investments to a small portion of their assets; another is created by subjecting the funds to extremely strict asset-allocation requirements, such as requiring a certain percentage of assets to be invested in domestic government bonds. For both pension and mutual funds, however, the prevalent regulatory view appears to be that prudential portfolio regulation should be based on broader principles that allow fund assets to be managed in an effective and efficient manner and, at the same time, ensure adequate protection of investors and policyholders.[22]

General Anticompetitive Measures. Trading partners may also wish to use the financial services negotiations in the Doha round to press for the reduction or elimination of other anticompetitive, nondiscriminatory structural barriers, regardless of whether their impact is to keep foreign firms from competing in a host-country market. Prior to enactment of U.S. financial services modernization legislation in 1999, for example, the European Union used the WTO, as well as other international and bilateral fora, to urge the United States to repeal Glass-Steagall Act restrictions separating commercial and investment banking and the Bank Holding Company Act prohibition on affiliations between banks and insurance companies.[23] Moreover, as part of the 1997 agreement, the U.S. administration made a "best efforts" additional commitment to try to work with Congress to achieve Glass-Steagall reform (see chapter 3).

Beyond "best efforts" commitments to remove general anticompetitive barriers, however, it is not clear that there is a compelling reason to bind the substantive elements of the resulting liberalization in the GATS. In the financial services sector, such liberalization often involves an extensive and complex set of changes to domestic legal frameworks that could not readily be bound as additional commitments in the GATS. Moreover, some measures would almost inevitably need to be modified over time as experience is gained with new structures or in light of new market developments. Even though such changes would presumably be for prudential reasons and fall within the prudential carve-out, countries would not want to make binding international commitments subject to WTO dispute settlement that might constrain their ability to modify their overall domestic financial structure. Strong first-pillar commitments to national treatment and market access are, of course, essential to ensure that foreign services and service providers benefit fully from a host country's existing domestic structure.

"Necessity" and Domestic Regulation. Article VI of the GATS (Domestic Regulation) provides a mandate for negotiating disciplines that would ensure that domestic standards and licensing requirements are not "more burdensome than necessary to ensure the quality of the service."[24] Beyond transparency and other procedural principles, however, the issues become much more difficult. It remains to be seen whether a widely applicable and mandatory necessity or least-trade-restrictive test for domestic regulation of services could ever be defined in the GATS in a manner that would not be unacceptably intrusive. In any event, for prudential measures, the prudential carve-out would override such a test. The only issues are whether the measure is, in fact, prudential, and whether it is being used to avoid a country's obligations or commitments under the GATS (see chapter 3).

Even if a widely applicable and mandatory necessity or least-trade-restrictive test could somehow be agreed upon in the GATS, its subsequent application to individual nonquantitative and nondiscriminatory structural measures through the WTO dispute settlement mechanism could open a Pandora's box of legal claims and counterclaims. By contrast, the effective-market-access approach discussed in this chapter is more pragmatic because it involves reaching a negotiated agreement among WTO members on individual measures to be covered by additional commitments. Trading partners are thereby forced to identify *ex ante* which domestic measures are so restrictive that they keep foreign service suppliers from competing in a host-country market; to determine whether there is a prevalent regulatory view that the measures cannot be justified on prudential grounds; and to try to convince the host country to accept that view.

Recognition of Prudential Measures

Differences in prudential rules among nations may unavoidably give rise to barriers to trade in financial services. Moreover, any efforts to reduce these barriers must avoid jeopardizing the goals these rules are designed to achieve. One approach to dealing with such barriers involves host-country recognition of home-country prudential measures. Indeed, acceptance of home-country rules and supervision, together with harmonization of essential rules, is the basis of the EU single-market program for the financial sector. Outside the European Union, however, few recognition arrangements exist for financial services.[25] Moreover, the German finance ministry's recognition of U.S. regulation and supervision that was discussed in chapter 4 was used to provide relief from a barrier that is inconsistent with national treatment and market access—namely, operating limits based on branch dotation capital requirements—as opposed to a nondiscriminatory barrier associated with differences in prudential rules among countries.

To facilitate recognition arrangements, the GATS Annex on Financial Services permits a departure from the MFN obligation for unilateral or mutual recognition of prudential measures. This provision allows a country to recognize prudential measures of selected other countries, either unilaterally or through a negotiated arrangement or agreement, without being subject to a challenge by an excluded WTO member that it is being denied MFN treatment. A country must, however, be willing to accord similar recognition to measures of other WTO members that meet the same standards.[26] In effect, the recognition provision in the Annex elaborates on the application to the financial services sector of Article VII of the GATS (Recognition), which allows a country to recognize standards or licensing or certification requirements of selected countries without being subject to the MFN obligation of the GATS.[27]

Although the GATS is permissive regarding recognition arrangements for prudential measures, it is not the appropriate forum for their negotiation. The German recognition arrangement with the United States, for example, involved negotiations between supervisory authorities and took the form of an exchange of letters and a subsequent regulation issued by the German finance ministry.[28] This is consistent with the approach used for supervisory cooperation and information-sharing agreements, which typically take the form of a memorandum of understanding (MOU), a statement of cooperation, or an exchange of letters among supervisors.

Harmonization. In general, a recognition arrangement needs to be predicated on some degree of harmonization of the rules of the home and host countries. Such harmonization may have already occurred de facto or could be achieved as a result of negotiations.[29] Recognition could be facilitated by a country's adherence to international minimum standards and codes of good practices for prudential regulation and supervision (see chapter 3), but such adherence would not necessarily provide sufficient harmonization for recognition. For example, the host country may impose higher or additional standards on both domestic and foreign firms, or the home country may generally adhere to international minimum standards but introduce certain differences in its application of those standards. In addition, the host country might not be willing to recognize the home country's ongoing supervision as sufficiently effective. Indeed, one reason that recognition arrangements are relatively rare in the financial sector is the importance and difficulty of evaluating home-country supervisory practices.

Facilitating Access. The recognition provision in the Annex on Financial Services is separate from, and in addition to, the prudential carve-out. The prudential carve-out allows a host country to take prudential measures that may be inconsistent with its GATS obligations and commitments. Thus, a financial regulatory authority that had specific prudential concerns about, say, the condition of an individual bank, or banks from a particular country, could apply appropriate measures without regard to whether such measures were consistent with its national treatment and market access commitments or its MFN obligation.

By contrast, the purpose of the recognition provision is to facilitate access to a host-country market by endorsing a mechanism that can be used to alleviate prudential concerns of host-country regulators. Host-country recognition of the adequacy of home-country regulation and supervision could be used, as discussed in chapter 4, to provide relief from host-country regulatory requirements that are inconsistent with national treatment or market access. To deal with barriers created by differences in nondiscriminatory prudential measures, recognition of specific elements of home-country regulation and supervision could be used to determine whether an applicant has met a mandatory host-country licensing or registration requirement, or to provide a procedural "fast lane" for determining compliance with a host-country requirement.[30]

Even when an element of recognition is present in a host-country licensing process, however, it may not necessarily involve a standing determination about a particular home country as envisaged by the GATS. In the banking sector, in particular, when acting upon an application for a license, authorities typically apply prudential standards primarily on the basis of an evaluation of an individual banking organization, including how it is regulated and supervised by the home country. For example, in the United States, the Federal Reserve Board is required to determine, among other things, that a foreign bank seeking to establish a U.S. branch is subject to "comprehensive supervision or regulation on a consolidated basis" in the home country, or that the authorities are actively working toward such supervision, in order to approve the application.[31] Determinations of whether this mandatory requirement has been met do not, however, constitute unilateral U.S. "recognition" of home-country supervision under the GATS, because no standing determination is made for a particular country. The determinations in each case do, of course, build upon any previous evaluation of the home country's supervision of other individual applicants.

The Intra-EU Approach

Efforts to achieve second-pillar liberalization internationally raise the question of the extent to which the EU approach to liberalization and regulation of trade in financial services among its member states might be applicable beyond the European Union. The EU single-market program is, in effect, an effort to achieve "EU contestability of markets" by dealing with all three pillars of liberalization: national treatment and market access; removal of nondiscriminatory structural barriers; and freedom of capital movements. Moreover, the EU single-market legislation includes most of the areas covered by the international work on strengthening domestic financial systems.

To remove nondiscriminatory structural barriers, including those associated with prudential measures, the EU uses the approach of "mutual recognition" and "home-country control." Mutual recognition involves harmonization of essential rules and acceptance of the rules of the home member state where harmonization has not occurred or has occurred only in general terms; home-country control refers to reliance on home-country supervision. The result is that a financial firm incorporated in any member state may provide services across borders or through the establishment of branches throughout the European Economic Area (EEA) on the basis of a "single license" issued by the home country.[32] Specifically, such services may be provided under home-country rules and supervision (referred to as the "home-country approach"), subject to the harmonization of essential rules required by EU legislation.

Reaching political agreement on goals for regulatory convergence and legislated harmonization of minimum standards are critical elements in the EU approach. De facto harmonization resulting from market forces also plays an important role by building upon and facilitating the home-country approach and the legislated harmonization. In addition, various sector-specific fora for banking, securities, and insurance facilitate cooperation and coordination with regard to regulation and supervision and, together with negotiated arrangements among supervisory authorities of the member states, play an important role in making the home-country approach work.[33]

Remaining Second-Pillar Barriers. Significant second-pillar barriers to a single market for financial services remain. Many of these barriers involve the "general good" exception to the home-country approach, under which a host member state may, subject to criteria established by the Court of Justice of the European Communities, apply its own rules on a national treatment basis for "imperative reasons relating to the general good."[34]

Invoking this exception, member states have retained numerous host-country rules—such as limitations on solicitation—that create significant, although nondiscriminatory, barriers to intra-EU trade in financial services. In addition, where sufficient harmonization could not be agreed upon to make the home-country approach acceptable to member states, some EU directives retain elements of the host-country approach.[35]

The introduction of the euro has given a new impetus to the removal of remaining barriers to a single market for financial services.[36] In June 1999, the Cologne European Council endorsed the European Commission's Financial Services Action Plan to improve the single market for financial services; subsequent European Councils in Lisbon and Stockholm set 2005 as the deadline for full implementation of the plan and the end of 2003 as a goal for legislation aimed at achieving an integrated securities market.[37] Work on the action plan focuses on three areas: (1) completing a single wholesale market; (2) developing "open and secure" markets for retail services, where progress has been much slower than for wholesale services; and (3) ensuring the continued stability of EU financial markets through enhancements to prudential rules and increased supervisory cooperation.[38]

The treatment of wholesale and retail financial services as separate areas reflects the strong concerns of member states about protecting retail customers, particularly with regard to cross-border services.[39] Such concerns have made it very difficult to reach agreement on liberalization in this area based on the home-country approach and harmonization of minimum standards.[40] Indeed, the EU experience highlights the challenges that must be faced in designing rules to govern cross-border trade in retail financial services beyond the single market.

Applicability of the Intra-EU Approach. The EU approach of mutual recognition and home-country control for removing second-pillar barriers would be difficult to apply generally to international trade in financial services. The main reason is that the EU single-market program has been undertaken within the unique supranational legislative, judicial, and administrative structure of the European Community, to which member states have transferred a significant degree of sovereignty.[41] In addition, within that supranational framework, the legislated harmonization of essential rules covers a broad range of areas. The so-called Codified Banking Directive, for example, deals with permissible activities and geographic expansion under the single license as well as prudential regulation and supervision, including capital requirements, large exposures, qualifying holdings outside the financial sector, and consolidated supervision.[42] Additional EU banking legislation deals with deposit insurance, bankruptcy rules, accounting, consumer credit, distance marketing, e-money, payment systems, and money laundering.[43] EU measures in other areas, such as competition policy and company law, also affect the financial sector.

6

Conclusion

—≈≈≈—

Financial services liberalization under the GATS is one part of the larger process of achieving international contestability of markets and strengthening domestic financial systems, including prudential regulation and supervision. The financial services negotiations in the Doha round offer an important opportunity to contribute to this effort by supporting and building upon political and market forces for liberalization and by obtaining binding commitments subject to the WTO dispute settlement mechanism. To use this opportunity most effectively, negotiations should (a) concentrate on fundamental first-pillar liberalization to obtain stronger and broader commitments for national treatment and market access and (b) focus on areas of second-pillar liberalization in which the GATS and the WTO have a comparative advantage. To this end, this study has identified six broad goals for the negotiations.

Four of the goals involve first-pillar liberalization aimed at achieving national treatment and market access:

1. Binding existing and ongoing liberalization that provides national treatment and market access to foreign financial services and service suppliers
2. Removing remaining barriers to national treatment and market access and then binding the resulting liberalization
3. Narrowing or withdrawing broad MFN exemptions, which are closely related to national treatment and market access commitments
4. Using an incremental approach for cross-border services that combines strengthening commitments and achieving greater liberalization in practice

The fifth and sixth goals involve second-pillar liberalization aimed at removing nonquantitative and nondiscriminatory structural barriers:

5. Developing stronger disciplines on regulatory transparency and the closely related issue of procedural fairness in applying regulations
6. Removing barriers that cannot be justified on prudential grounds and serve primarily to deny "effective market access" to foreign service suppliers, and then binding the resulting liberalization

These second-pillar goals reflect the view that the financial services negotiations in the Doha round should proceed selectively in going beyond national treatment and market access. Strengthened GATS disciplines on regulatory transparency and procedural fairness could both complement and build upon the work on transparency that is part of the international effort to strengthen domestic financial systems. Such disciplines could not only reduce or eliminate nondiscriminatory structural barriers created by opaque and unfair regulatory procedures, but also play a critical role in helping to ensure that commitments to national treatment and market access are honored in practice. GATS commitments dealing with barriers to effective market access would go one step beyond national treatment and market access by focusing on nondiscriminatory structural measures that cannot be justified on prudential grounds and serve primarily to keep foreign service suppliers from competing in host-country markets by making entry impractical or too costly.

Barriers to trade in financial services can also be created by legitimate prudential rules, that is, measures to promote the integrity and stability of the financial system or to protect consumers of financial services. The prudential carve-out ensures that a WTO member may take such measures even if they are inconsistent with its obligations and commitments in the GATS. The international work on minimum standards and codes of good practices for prudential regulation and supervision provides general guidance on the areas in which prudential regulation is appropriate and on the types of rules that are widely accepted as legitimate prudential measures. Against this background, pressure from a country's trading partners—and, for particularly egregious measures, use of the WTO dispute settlement mechanism—will need to be relied upon to prevent abuse of the prudential carve-out.

Recognition arrangements can be used to deal with nondiscriminatory structural barriers that arise from differences in prudential rules among countries, as well as to provide relief from prudential rules that are inconsistent with national treatment and market access. Although the GATS facilitates recognition arrangements, their negotiation is beyond its purview. Success in using recognition arrangements to deal with barriers created by differences in prudential measures requires some degree of regulatory convergence, either de facto or through negotiated harmonization. Such convergence requires an implicit or explicit consensus between home and host countries on whether particular measures are "reasonable" or "necessary." The EU experience with the single-market program for the financial sector highlights the difficulties of reaching such a consensus even within the unique supranational structure of the European Community. These difficulties are particularly acute with regard to consumer protection measures for retail financial services provided across borders, which may occur increasingly through the Internet.

Concerns about ensuring consumer protection for retail financial services provided in cyberspace remain an important factor in the reluctance of OECD countries to make binding commitments to national treatment and market access in the GATS—even for existing liberalization—for a broad range of financial services provided through mode 1 (cross-border supply). This study therefore suggests—as part of an incremental approach to strengthening commitments for cross-border services—trying to obtain mode 1 commitments to national treatment and market access for services that present the fewest risks to retail customers or, for some services, covering wholesale customers only. National treatment, while extremely important, is only a threshold issue for cross-border services. A much more difficult issue is the extent to which host countries, beyond the intra-EU single market, may increasingly need to rely on home-country regulation and supervision of financial services provided across national borders.

Success in achieving the financial services goals discussed in this study depends significantly on factors beyond the scope of the negotiations. As the GATS explicitly recognizes, liberalization of trade in financial and other services is an ongoing process. For financial services, this process is being driven in large part by market forces and new technologies. It is also being driven by the growing recognition among policymakers that market opening can benefit host-country consumers of financial services and, at the same time, contribute to the resiliency of domestic financial systems. The development of international minimum standards and codes of good practices for sound financial systems and their implementation by individual countries provides a strong foundation for moving ahead with further liberalization of trade in financial services. The negotiations in the Doha round can play an important role in helping to accelerate the process of liberalization as well as solidifying its results in the form of binding commitments subject to the WTO dispute settlement mechanism.

Notes

—∞∞∞—

Chapter 1: Introduction

1. GATS, art. XIX, para. 1.

2. Although the Final Act Embodying the Results of the Uruguay Round of Multilateral Trade Negotiations was signed in April 1994, the negotiations on the GATS and other Uruguay Round agreements were completed in December 1993. See World Trade Organization (1995).

3. See Key (1997) and Kono et al. (1997). The schedules of commitments agreed upon in December 1997 were incorporated into the GATS by the Fifth Protocol to the GATS, which entered into force on March 1, 1999 (see chap. 4, n. 1).

4. See World Trade Organization (2001e), para. 15. Negotiations on agriculture were also part of the "built-in" agenda that was established in the Uruguay Round. See Agreement on Agriculture, art. 20.

5. See World Trade Organization (2001e), para. 45. In this study, the term "Doha round" refers to the multilateral trade negotiations that are part of the "Doha Development Agenda." Because of objections by a number of countries, particularly emerging market economies and other developing countries, the Doha Ministerial Declaration did not designate the negotiations as the "Doha Round." The WTO is referring to the trade negotiations, in combination with other elements of the work program agreed upon in Doha, as the "Doha Development Agenda." These other elements include: (a) work on the decision on implementation, which addresses the problems developing countries face in implementing the current WTO agreements; and (b) analysis, in anticipation of future negotiations, in areas such as the relationship between trade and investment, the interaction of trade and competition policy, and transparency in government procurement. See World Trade Organization (2001c, 2001e).

6. See chap. 3, n. 45, regarding the Basel Committee on Banking Supervision.

7. See International Monetary Fund (2002b).

8. See International Monetary Fund (2001a, 2001c, 2002b).

9. GATS, art. II, para. 1. The GATS allows certain departures from the MFN obligation. See chap. 1, n. 12, and accompanying text regarding economic integration agreements. In addition, subject to certain conditions, the GATS allows one-time exemptions from the MFN obligation to be taken upon entry into force of a country's

61

initial schedule of commitments under the GATS (see chapter 4). Moreover, the MFN obligation does not apply to recognition of standards or licensing or certification requirements (see chapter 5 regarding recognition of prudential measures).

10. The GATS does not cover services supplied in the exercise of governmental authority—for example, in the activities of central banks or monetary authorities in pursuit of monetary or exchange rate policies. In addition, at present, measures relating to government procurement of services fall outside the scope of the MFN, market access, and national treatment provisions of the GATS. Further work in this area, which is required by the GATS, is still in its early stages. Most of the countries belonging to the Organization for Economic Cooperation and Development (OECD), however, have already committed, in accordance with the Understanding on Commitments in Financial Services (see chap. 3, n. 8), to provide both MFN and national treatment with respect to government procurement of financial services. (As of January 2003, the OECD had thirty members: Australia, Austria, Belgium, Canada, the Czech Republic, Denmark, Finland, France, Germany, Greece, Hungary, Iceland, Ireland, Italy, Japan, Korea, Luxembourg, Mexico, the Netherlands, New Zealand, Norway, Poland, Portugal, the Slovak Republic, Spain, Sweden, Switzerland, Turkey, the United Kingdom, and the United States.)

11. See chap. 3, n. 19, regarding the distinction between the European Community (EC) and the European Union (EU).

12. To qualify for this exception, an agreement must have substantial sectoral coverage that does not exclude a priori any mode of supply (see chapter 2); must provide for the absence or elimination of substantially all discrimination incompatible with national treatment among the parties; and must not raise the overall level of barriers to trade in services within the respective sectors or subsectors. For agreements among developing countries, the GATS provides for flexibility in meeting these conditions, especially the elimination of "substantially all discrimination." See GATS, art. V (Economic Integration). A further limited exception from the MFN obligation is allowed for agreements establishing full integration of labor markets. See GATS, art. V bis (Labor Markets Integration Agreements).

13. For example, if the OECD countries (see chap. 1, n. 10) had succeeded in their attempt in the late 1990s to negotiate an investment agreement among themselves, the MFN obligation in the GATS would, in general, have required any additional liberalization of investment in services under that agreement to be extended to all WTO members.

Chapter 2: International Trade in Financial Services

1. See Levine (1996) for a detailed discussion of the role of the financial system. See also Dobson and Jacquet (1998).

2. See Kono et al. (1997), Dobson and Jacquet (1998), Claessens, Demirgüç-Kunt, and Huizinga (1998), Claessens and Glaessner (1997), Levine (1996), and World Trade Organization (2000a).

3. See Kono et al. (1997), chapter 3, for a discussion of the "remarkable" lack of reliable and detailed data on international trade in financial services and a comprehensive analysis of the available statistics. See also World Trade Organization (1998a). See Hawkins and Mihaljek (2001), p. 24, and Table 8, for data on the foreign bank presence in selected emerging market economies. See Organization for Economic Cooperation and Development (2000) for a discussion of general trends in cross-border financial services.

4. The country in which the office of the financial firm is "located" could be either the country in which it is headquartered or a third country in which it has a branch or subsidiary.

5. More generally, foreign direct investment involves an ongoing interest in and influence over the management of a commercial enterprise in another country. The threshold used for defining foreign direct investment in balance-of-payments accounting by the United States and most other countries, which is contained in the IMF's Balance-of-Payments Manual, is 10 percent ownership or control of an enterprise's voting shares. (By contrast, portfolio investment consists of the ownership of securities where the 10 percent threshold is not met, and often consists of short-term activity in financial markets.) In balance-of-payments accounting, branches of foreign firms (which are not separately incorporated in the host country) are, in general, treated as if they were wholly owned subsidiaries. Some foreign direct investment may take the form of a "joint venture"—that is, a business operation that two or more firms undertake together. See United Nations Conference on Trade and Development and the World Bank (1994), International Monetary Fund (1993), and U.S. Department of Commerce (1990). See chap. 2, n. 22 regarding the types of foreign direct investment covered by the GATS.

6. See Karsenty (2000).

7. See Skipper (2001).

8. The GATS Annex on Financial Services defines a financial service as "any service of a financial nature offered by a financial service supplier of a [WTO] Member." It also specifies that "[f]inancial services include all insurance and insurance-related services, and all banking and other financial services (excluding insurance)." The Annex contains a nonexclusive list of activities included in this definition of financial services that is a slightly modified version of the WTO Services Sectoral Classification List used during the Uruguay Round negotiations (known as the "W120 list"). A firm or individual "wishing to supply or supplying financial services" falls within the GATS definition of a financial service supplier and can benefit from the GATS regime for financial services. See GATS Annex on Financial Services, para. 5. See also United Nations Conference on

Trade and Development and World Bank (1994), Whichard (2001), and World Trade Organization (1998a) regarding the WTO Services Sectoral Classification List.

9. For a number of countries that participated actively in the negotiations on banking and other financial services, finance officials played a major role as negotiators, although trade officials retained overall responsibility. By contrast, insurance was handled almost exclusively by trade officials.

10. There is no generally accepted definition of wholesale customers. For example, some regulations that distinguish between retail and wholesale customers do not include wealthy individuals in the wholesale category. See Financial Services Authority [UK] (2001b).

11. See Sato and Hawkins (2001), Wenninger (2000), and Claessens, Glaessner, and Klingebiel (2000).

12. See "Going for Brokers" (2000), Sato and Hawkins (2001), and Claessens, Glaessner, and Klingebiel (2000).

13. In the banking sector, even if the host country permits direct branches of foreign banks to conduct a retail as well as a wholesale business, direct branches engaging in retail activities are usually located in areas with a large concentration of residents with ties to the home country.

14. For instance, some countries, such as Australia and Japan, permit the cross-border sale to domestic residents of mutual funds registered in certain jurisdictions, including the United States. Because of tax barriers, however, domestic residents may not want to purchase such funds. Income from domestic funds may receive more favorable tax treatment, for example, or requirements under home-country tax law (such as that of the United States) for distribution of capital gains may not be attractive to host-country investors if domestic funds are not subject to such requirements. In Australia, taxable distributions are required for domestic funds; for mutual funds purchased across borders, Australian tax law requires imputing tax on the basis of the appreciation of each fund's portfolio to prevent residents from deferring payment of Australian tax. Australian recognition of U.S. tax law with respect to required distributions from mutual funds has, however, facilitated the purchase of U.S. mutual funds by Australian residents (see chap. 5, n. 25).

15. As a legal matter, in terms of scheduling commitments in the GATS, providing services via the Internet need not be treated differently than providing services via telephone or fax. Some commentators have emphasized the importance of explicitly confirming this principle of "technological neutrality" in the GATS to ensure that members would not make policy distinctions among services based on the technological means of delivery. See Mattoo and Schuknecht (2000).

16. The issue of clarifying the distinction between mode 1 and mode 2 in the GATS may be raised during the Doha round services negotiations. One approach would be

to define mode 2 to require the physical presence of the consumer in the country of the service supplier; another approach (which appears to have little, if any, support among WTO members) would be to combine the two modes. See Mattoo and Schuknecht (2000). In view of the difficulties in distinguishing between the two modes, some WTO members who used the Understanding on Commitments in Financial Services (see chap. 3, n. 8 and n.14) to make commitments in mode 2 (consumption abroad) for a broad range of financial services (see chap. 4) included statements in the so-called headnotes to their financial services schedules emphasizing that these commitments did not require them to allow solicitation by foreign service suppliers. See World Trade Organization (1996a).

17. See Key and Scott (1991) and Financial Services Authority [UK](2001a).

18. In this example, the question would be whether the activity rises to the level of a representative office. In economic terms, a foreign bank's representative office—which is normally not legally permitted to sign loan or deposit contracts—is basically a marketing mechanism used to facilitate the cross-border provision of financial services. In the GATS, however, the definition of "commercial presence" includes representative offices (see chap. 2, n. 22).

19. For example, under U.S. Securities and Exchange Commission (SEC) regulations, foreign broker-dealers cannot, in general, solicit business from U.S. residents without triggering the U.S. broker-dealer registration requirement. Securities and Exchange Commission Rule 15a-6. 17 C.F.R. § 240 (2002). Also available at www.law.uc.edu/CCL/34ActRls/rule15a-6.html (accessed January 2003).

20. See International Organization of Securities Commissions (1998, 2001), U.S. Securities and Exchange Commission (1997), Financial Services Authority [UK] (1998, 2001a), and Mann and Carney (2002).

21. See Financial Services Authority [UK] (2001a).

22. "Establishment of a commercial presence" in the GATS includes foreign direct investment in the form of a branch of a foreign financial firm or an entity that is majority-owned or controlled by a foreign firm or individual; entities that are majority-owned or controlled jointly by two or more foreign owners would also be included. Majority-ownership or control by another company is the definition of a "subsidiary" that is generally used for financial accounting purposes. "Establishment" of a subsidiary under the GATS could occur through the acquisition of shares of either an existing or de novo company in the host country. The GATS definition of a commercial presence also includes representative offices, which are basically a marketing device and do not constitute foreign direct investment (see chap. 2, n. 18). The Understanding on Commitments in Financial Services, which was used by most OECD countries to supplement the requirements of the GATS framework agreement (see chap. 3, n. 8), defines a commercial presence more explicitly and somewhat more broadly to include "wholly- or partly-owned subsidiaries, joint ventures, partnerships, sole proprietorships, franchising operations, branches, agencies, representative offices

or other organizations" (Understanding on Commitments in Financial Services, para. D.2). In any event, even if a WTO member has limited its market access commitment in financial services to a level of foreign ownership that would be noncontrolling, the market access commitment per se is still a binding commitment subject to enforcement through the WTO dispute settlement mechanism. However, because the foreign owner would not fall within the GATS definition of a foreign service supplier, arguably other provisions of the GATS might not apply. See GATS art. XXVIII (Definitions).

23. The Agreement on Trade-Related Investment Measures (TRIMs) applies to certain conditions placed on investment that have an impact on trade in goods, such as local content requirements or trade-balancing requirements.

24. In the NAFTA, the investment chapter does not apply to measures to the extent that they are covered by the financial services chapter; however, the financial services chapter incorporates certain provisions from the investment chapter. See North American Free Trade Agreement (1992), chapters 11, 14.

25. In the financial services sector, natural persons, with the exception of financial advisors (and, in insurance, independent sales intermediaries), virtually always provide services as employees of financial firms rather than as individual service suppliers.

26. The scope of commitments for the temporary presence of natural persons is governed by a separate annex. See GATS, Annex on Movement of Natural Persons Supplying Services under the Agreement.

27. These commitments are set forth in the Understanding on Commitments in Financial Services (see chap. 3, n. 8). For a list of the OECD member countries, see chap. 1, n. 10.

Chapter 3: Liberalization and Regulation

1. See Key (1999).

2. GATS Annex on Financial Services, para. 2.

3. See Beviglia Zampetti and Sauvé (1996), Graham and Lawrence (1996), and Lawrence (1996).

4. See Gianviti (1999b), Holder (1999), and Leckow (2000) regarding the role of the IMF in liberalization of capital movements.

5. This section and the following section on nondiscriminatory structural barriers draw upon Key (1997).

6. See World Trade Organization (2001a) and Morris (2001) regarding economic needs tests.

7. Use of the broad term "treatment no less favorable" has the effect of requiring both *de jure* and *de facto* national treatment. Moreover, it does not necessarily

require precisely identical treatment of domestic and foreign services and service suppliers. See GATS, art. XVII.

8. The Understanding on Commitments in Financial Services, however, sets forth a broad commitment to the right of establishment or expansion of a commercial presence (see chapter 4). The Understanding provides an alternative approach to scheduling commitments that was used by most of the OECD countries to supplement the requirements of the GATS framework agreement. In effect, the Understanding is a model schedule, albeit a particularly complicated one. In legal terms, the Understanding is incorporated by reference into the GATS through the schedules of commitments of the countries that use it. Commitments scheduled under the Understanding are extended to all members of the WTO regardless of whether the members schedule commitments under the framework or the Understanding. See Key (1997) and, for the legal text, World Trade Organization (1995); see also chap. 3, n. 14.

9. See Hoekman (1996) and Mattoo (1997). Article XX of the GATS (Schedules of Specific Commitments), which deals with scheduling of commitments, explicitly refers to cases in which a measure is inconsistent with both market access and national treatment. It provides that such measures should be listed as limitations under market access and states that they will be considered limitations under national treatment as well. See GATS, art. XX, para. 2.

10. In the GATT, by contrast, national treatment is a general obligation applicable to all products.

11. In scheduling financial services commitments, some WTO members listed such narrow "subsectors"—for example, "acceptance of deposits and other repayable funds from the public"—that they are, in effect, lists of activities.

12. Limitations are, however, listed separately for each mode of supply (see chapter 2); therefore, a member could—even for a listed sector, subsector, or activity—avoid making any commitments for an entire mode of supply by simply entering the term "unbound." See chap. 4, n. 7, and Key (1997).

13. See Low and Mattoo (2000), Hoekman (1996), and Hoekman and Sauvé (1994).

14. This approach is referred to as a "top down" or "negative list" approach to scheduling commitments. In its most stringent form, a negative list would mean that only nonconforming measures could be listed as exceptions to national treatment or market access; "negative list" is widely used, however, to refer to an approach that would also allow a country to take exceptions for particular sectors, subsectors, or activities. See Low and Mattoo (2000). The GATS approach to scheduling commitments is referred to as a "hybrid list" because it involves a so-called "positive list" of sectors, subsectors, and activities for which commitments are undertaken and, within each listed sector, subsector, or activity, a "negative list" of limitations on national treatment or market access. See Key (1997) for a comparison of "negative lists" and GATS "hybrid lists." The Understanding on

Commitments in Financial Services (see chap. 3, n. 8) uses, in effect, a negative list approach to scheduling financial services commitments in mode 3 (establishment of a commercial presence) and mode 2 (consumption abroad). Countries using the Understanding undertake commitments to national treatment and market access—under the GATS framework agreement as supplemented by the Understanding—for all financial services in these modes, except for nonconforming measures listed in their schedules or measures that fall within the scope of the prudential carve-out or the other public policy exceptions in the GATS.

15. The Gramm-Leach-Bliley Act of 1999, Pub. L. No. 106-102, 113 Stat. 1338 (1999), authorizes affiliations among banks, securities firms, insurance firms, and other financial companies provided that the banks are well-capitalized and well-managed. Previously, the Bank Holding Company Act, as amended by the Garn-St.Germain Depository Institutions Act of 1982, had specifically prohibited U.S. bank holding companies (including their nonbanking subsidiaries) from engaging in most insurance activities in the United States.

16. In many countries, asset-management services are subject to overlapping regulatory regimes for securities and pension fund regulation. In the United States, for example, entities providing asset-management services are, in general, regulated under the securities laws by the Securities and Exchange Commission. (A limited exception is provided for certain asset-management activities conducted by banks.) If the entity is also providing asset-management services to a pension fund, the fund is subject to the regulatory regime established by the Employee Retirement Income Security Act of 1974 (ERISA), and the asset-management firm is subject to the requirements of ERISA as well as the securities laws.

17. See Investment Company Institute (2001).

18. The GATS provides an exception to national treatment to ensure that governments may treat foreign and domestic taxpayers differently, provided that the difference in treatment is "aimed at ensuring the equitable or effective imposition or collection of direct taxes." The GATS also allows WTO members to take actions that are inconsistent with the MFN obligation provided that the difference in treatment among countries is the result of provisions on the avoidance of double taxation in any international agreement or arrangement by which the country is bound.

19. The European Community (EC), which was formerly the European Economic Community (EEC), and the European Atomic Energy Community (Euratom) constitute the supranational "first pillar" of the European Union (EU). Prior to July 24, 2002, the European Coal and Steel Community (ECSC), which expired fifty years after its entry into force, was the third Community under the EU's "first pillar." The EU was created by the Treaty on European Union (TEU), often referred to as the Maastricht Treaty, which entered into force on November 1, 1993. The EU's "second pillar" (common foreign and security policy) and "third pillar" (police and judicial cooperation in criminal matters) are both intergovernmental. From a legal point

of view, the two European Communities (not the EU itself) and their member states are members of the WTO. The reason is that the area of trade is governed by the two Community treaties (the EC Treaty and the Euratom Treaty), which the Maastricht Treaty amended but did not replace. For simplicity and in accordance with generally accepted nontechnical usage, "European Union" or "EU" is used in this study except when it is necessary to refer to the European Community or the European Communities as specific legal entities.

20. GATS, art. III, para. 1.

21. GATS, art. VI, para. 1.

22. See GATS, art. VI, para. 2.

23. Initial work under this mandate has led to adoption of disciplines on domestic regulation in the accountancy sector, which are scheduled to enter into force no later than the conclusion of the Doha round. See L. White (2001).

24. See World Trade Organization (1996b).

25. See Hoekman (1997) and Hoekman, Low, and Mavroidis (1996).

26. This general best-efforts commitment is contained in the Understanding on Commitments in Financial Services. See chap. 3, n. 8.

27. Capital assets comprise intangible assets (which, in addition to financial assets, include intellectual property) and real estate. A capital transaction is always considered "international" if it takes place between a resident and a nonresident. A broader definition of "international" includes transactions between residents of the same country that involve a foreign capital asset. See International Monetary Fund (1993).

28. See Holder (1999).

29. See chap. 2, n. 5, regarding the definition of foreign direct investment and chap. 2, n. 22, regarding the coverage of foreign direct investment in the GATS.

30. See Eichengreen and Mussa with Dell'Ariccia et al. (1998), Fischer et al. (1998), Greenspan (1998), Krugman (1998), Sachs (1998), Stiglitz (1998), and Summers (1998a, 1998b).

31. See Rogoff (2002).

32. See Ishii and Habermeier (2002), W. White (2000), Eichengreen and Mussa with Dell'Ariccia et al. (1998), and Meyers (2001b).

33. Besides the creation or transfer of ownership of financial assets, international capital transactions associated with establishment of a commercial presence by a foreign financial firm could also involve the purchase of real estate.

34. Under standard balance-of-payments accounting, however, even if the earnings of the subsidiary were reinvested, they would be regarded as additional foreign direct investment by the parent in the subsidiary. See International Monetary Fund (1993) and U.S. Department of Commerce (1990).

35. Branches are often *net* recipients of funds from the head office, although some branches that raise funds in host-country money markets are *net* suppliers of funds to the head office.

36. Equity and permanent debt investment (i.e., loan capital representing a permanent interest) of the head office in the branch are classified in the balance-of-payments as foreign direct investment; debt investment of the head office in the branch that is not permanent and debt claims of the branch on its head office are classified as portfolio investment. See U.S. Department of Commerce (1990) and International Monetary Fund (1993). The balance-of-payments concept of branch capital is separate and distinct from the *regulatory* capital-equivalency requirements that a number of host countries apply to branches (see chapter 4).

37. The capital transaction in these examples—that is, the transfer of ownership of the underlying instrument—would be international if the new owner were a resident of a different country than the previous owner; the broader definition would include transactions where the owners were residents of the same country but the instrument had been originally issued in another country (see chap. 3, n. 27).

38. Exceptions are provided for restrictions imposed under Article XII (Restrictions to Safeguard the Balance of Payments) or at the request of the IMF. See GATS, art. XI, para. 2. Article XI also requires WTO members not to impose restrictions on payments and transfers associated with current transactions. See GATS, art. XI, para. 1.

39. GATS, art. XVI, n. 8. "Essential" effectively limits the first requirement to the financial services sector. By contrast, "related" would apply the second requirement to all services sectors; outward capital movements were not covered because of concern on the part of some members about "capital flight."

40. The GATS balance-of-payments safeguard allows a WTO member to impose temporary restrictions that suspend its commitments in the event of "serious balance-of-payments and external financial difficulties or threat thereof." Besides being temporary, such restrictions must adhere to the most favored nation (MFN) principle; be consistent with the IMF Articles of Agreement; not exceed those necessary to deal with the circumstances; and avoid unnecessary damage to the commercial, economic, and financial interests of other WTO members. Members invoking the balance-of-payments safeguard are required to consult with the WTO Committee on Balance-of-Payments Restrictions. See GATS, art. XII (Restrictions to Safeguard the Balance of Payments).

41. The IMF articles of agreement do not include liberalization of capital movements as an objective; moreover, if necessary, they allow the imposition of capital controls. Even under the existing articles, however, the Fund is heavily involved with capital movements as part of its responsibility for oversight of the international monetary system, in its routine surveillance of economic policies of its members (so-called Article IV surveillance), and in its stabilization programs, which, subject to conditions, provide financing for balance-of-payments purposes. As the Asian financial crisis was developing, active consideration was being given to amending the IMF Articles of Agreement to extend its formal jurisdiction with respect to capital movements. The crisis made these discussions more

difficult, and work on amending the articles was discontinued. See Fischer et al. (1998), Gianviti (1999b), Hagan (1999), Holder (1999), and Leckow (2000).

42. The *Group of Seven* (G-7) consists of Canada, France, Germany, Italy, Japan, the United Kingdom, and the United States. Summit meetings are held annually, and finance ministers and central bank governors meet several times a year to discuss national economic policies, exchange rate developments, and other global economic issues. During the 1990s, Russia was gradually integrated into the summit process, and the *Group of Eight* (G-8) was established in 1998. Financial issues, however, continue to be dealt with separately in the G-7 finance ministers' channel. The *Group of Ten* (G-10), which serves as a policy forum in which central bank governors play a leading role, actually comprises eleven countries: Belgium, Canada, France, Germany, Italy, Japan, the Netherlands, Sweden, Switzerland, the United Kingdom, and the United States. The *Group of Twenty* (G-20), established in 1999, is a forum for finance ministers and central bank governors of nineteen countries— the G-7 countries plus twelve additional systemically important countries (Argentina, Australia, Brazil, China, India, Indonesia, Korea, Mexico, Russia, Saudi Arabia, South Africa, and Turkey)—and representatives of the European Union (the country holding the presidency, if not a G-7 member, and the European Central Bank); the IMF and the World Bank also participate. The *Financial Stability Forum* (FSF), established by the G-7 in 1999, brings together on a regular basis representatives of national authorities responsible for financial stability in eleven significant international financial centers (the G-7 plus Australia, Hong Kong, the Netherlands, and Singapore), international financial institutions, sector-specific international bodies dealing with regulatory and supervisory issues, committees of central bank experts, and the European Central Bank. The *Basel Committee on Banking Supervision* (Basel Committee) was set up by the central bank governors of the G-10 countries in 1975 in the aftermath of the failure of Bankhaus Herstatt in what was then West Germany; its secretariat is provided by the Bank for International Settlements (BIS). The membership of the Basel Committee includes central banks and non-central bank authorities responsible for banking supervision from the G-10 countries plus Luxembourg and Spain. The *International Organization of Securities Commissions* (IOSCO) is a worldwide membership organization created in 1983 and now headquartered in Madrid. In the insurance sector, the *International Association of Insurance Supervisors* (IAIS), which was established in 1994, comprises insurance supervisory authorities from more than 100 jurisdictions. See International Monetary Fund (2002a). See also www.g7.utoronto.ca, www.fin.gc.ca/g20/indexe. html, www.fsforum.org, www.bis.org/bcbs/index.htm, www.iosco.org, and www.iaisweb.org (accessed January 2003).

43. See W. White (1998).

44. See Financial Stability Forum (2002a).

45. See Basel Committee on Banking Supervision (1997). The Basel Core Principles were issued together with a compendium of rules and recommendations

on banking supervision that represents the previous two decades of work of the Basel Committee. For internationally active banks, the Basel Core Principles, in effect, incorporate the minimum standards established by the 1988 Basel Risk-based Capital Accord, which, as of this writing (January 2003), is in the process of an extensive revision. Documents produced by the Basel Committee are available on the BIS web site at www.bis.org/bcbs/index.htm (accessed January 2003).

46. Documents are available on the IOSCO web site, www.iosco.org (accessed January 2003).

47. See Lane et al. (1999).

48. Conthe and Ingves (2001). See also International Monetary Fund (2002d) and Financial Stability Forum (2002a).

49. Assessments conducted during 2001–02 typically covered, depending on the circumstances of an individual country, the IMF's Code of Good Practices on Transparency in Monetary and Financial Policies (see chapter 5), the Basel Core Principles, the IOSCO Objectives and Principles of Securities Regulation, the Insurance Core Principles, and the Core Principles for Systemically Important Payment Systems. The detailed FSAP work forms the basis of Financial System Stability Assessments (FSSAs) and Reports on the Observance of Standards and Codes for the financial sector, which are included in the FSSA reports. FSSAs, prepared by IMF staff, address issues relevant to the IMF's Article IV surveillance, such as risks to macroeconomic stability arising from the financial sector and the sector's capacity to absorb macroeconomic shocks; FSSA reports are published at the discretion of individual countries. The FSAP also forms the basis of Financial Sector Assessments (FSAs), prepared by World Bank staff, which focus on structural issues and capacity building needs; FSA reports are also published at the discretion of individual countries. See International Monetary Fund (2002d) and Financial Stability Forum (2002a).

50. See Conthe and Ingves (2001) and International Monetary Fund (2002d).

51. See Basel Committee on Banking Supervision (1999).

52. See Basel Committee on Banking Supervision (2001) regarding "supervisory self-assessments."

53. Even within the European Union, the European Central Bank (ECB) has only advisory and consultative powers in bank regulation and supervision. An enabling clause in the treaty would allow other powers to be transferred to the ECB, but such a transfer would require a unanimous decision by the Council of Economic and Finance Ministers (ECOFIN Council). See Treaty establishing the European Community (consolidated text), art. 105 (ex art. 105), paras. 5, 6. See also Protocol on the Statute of the European System of Central Banks and of the European Central Bank (annexed to the Treaty establishing the European Community by the Treaty on European Union), art. 25.

54. GATS, Annex on Financial Services, para. 2.

55. See GATS, art. XIV (General Exceptions). A separate exception for national security allows a member to take any action that the member considers necessary for the protection of its essential security interests. See GATS, art. XIV bis (National Security).

56. Some measures that fall within the scope of the prudential carve-out may also fall within the general domestic policy exceptions in Article XIV of the GATS (General Exceptions). For example, Article XIV provides an exception for adoption or enforcement of measures necessary to secure compliance with nondiscriminatory laws and regulations relating to the prevention of deceptive and fraudulent practices.

57. As of this writing (January 2003), there had been no dispute settlement proceeding and no request for consultation on a financial services issue.

58. Suppose, for example, that a member has scheduled commitments for financial services without taking any exception for an economic needs test but nonetheless imposes such a test on "prudential" grounds. It is difficult to see how such a measure could be anything other than an abuse of the prudential carve-out.

59. GATS, Annex on Financial Services, para. 4. This standard is more narrowly drawn than the general standard applicable to the GATS, which requires panels to have the "necessary expertise relevant to the specific services sectors which the dispute concerns." Decision on Certain Dispute Settlement Procedures for the General Agreement on Trade in Services, para. 4. World Trade Organization (1995).

Chapter 4: National Treatment and Market Access

1. See World Trade Organization (1997a, 1997b, 1999a, 1999b). For WTO members that participated in the 1997 negotiations but accepted the Fifth Protocol after March 1, 1999, commitments entered into force upon acceptance. The protocol initially remained open for acceptance until July 15, 1999; as of this writing (January 2003), it had been reopened for acceptance by Costa Rica and Nicaragua (late 1999), Ghana, Kenya, and Nigeria (2000), and Bolivia (2002).

2. This figure includes the European Communities as a single WTO member as well as the fifteen member states (see chap. 3, n. 19). Strictly speaking, only seventy members made *improved* or first-time commitments. The exception was Ecuador, which acceded to the WTO in 1996 and used the special rules governing the extended financial services negotiations to weaken its schedule by imposing a temporary freeze on new licenses for both domestic and foreign banks. (Bulgaria, which also acceded in 1996, further strengthened its schedule in 1997.) See British Invisibles (1998), Kampf (1998), and Mattoo (2000) regarding commitments made by individual countries. See U.S. Department of the Treasury (1998) and World Trade Organization (1998b) regarding improvements made in the 1997 schedules.

3. The six countries that participated in the 1997 negotiations but, as of January 2003, had not yet accepted the Fifth Protocol are Brazil, the Dominican Republic, Jamaica, the Philippines, Poland, and Uruguay.

4. As of January 1, 2003, sixteen members had acceded to the WTO through full accession negotiations under Article XII of the Marrakesh Agreement Establishing the World Trade Organization (as opposed to special GATT/WTO transitional arrangements): Bulgaria and Ecuador (1996), both of which participated in the 1997 negotiations and are therefore included with the Fifth Protocol countries; Mongolia and Panama (1997); Kyrgyz Republic (1998); Estonia and Latvia (1999); Albania, Croatia, Georgia, Jordan, and Oman (2000); Lithuania, Moldova, and China (2001); and Chinese Taipei (2002). (Accession packages of two additional countries—Armenia and Macedonia—were approved by the WTO General Council in late 2002; they will become members in 2003 after domestic ratification procedures have been completed.)

5. A notable exception is Argentina, which made generally strong commitments in 1993 and did not modify its schedule in 1997. Most of the countries in this group have commitments that have remained unchanged since either December 1993 (the end of the Uruguay Round negotiations) or July 1995 (the so-called interim agreement on financial services). This group also includes several smaller developing countries with minimal financial services commitments that acceded to the WTO in 1995 and 1996 under special GATT/WTO transitional arrangements. See Kampf (1995), Freiberg (1996), and Key (1997) regarding the interim agreement on financial services, the results of which are reflected in the Second Protocol to the GATS (S/L/11), the Decision adopting the Second Protocol to the GATS (S/L/13), the Decision on Commitments in Financial Services (S/L/8), and the Second Decision on Financial Services (S/L/9), available at http://docson line.wto.org (accessed January 2003).

6. Côte d'Ivoire made a first-time commitment in financial services in 1998.

7. The Marrakesh Agreement Establishing the World Trade Organization (WTO Agreement) provides that when a government accepts the WTO Agreement, it accepts all of the multilateral trade agreements that are annexed to it, including the GATS. (This acceptance of the multilateral agreements as a package is sometimes referred to as a "single undertaking.") See Agreement Establishing the World Trade Organization, art. XIV, para. 1. A WTO member must have schedules of commitments for goods and services; a services schedule may, however, include a commitment in only one services sector. Thus the sectoral coverage of services commitments varies widely. For example, in the Uruguay Round, a number of developing countries submitted services schedules covering only tourism. Even if a country does submit a schedule covering financial services, the commitments may be very limited—for example, commitments could cover only a few narrowly defined subsectors or activities and, within a listed subsector or activity, exclude one or more modes of supply or list other limitations on national treatment or market access. See chap. 3, n. 12, and Key (1997).

8. The European Communities and each member state are counted separately in these statistics; that is, they are counted as sixteen members. The total number of members with financial services commitments includes the six countries that had not accepted the Fifth Protocol as of January 2003 (see chap. 4, n. 3), because each of these countries had previous commitments in force. Financial services commitments made by each WTO member are available at http://doc sonline.wto.org (accessed January 2003).

9. The GATS negotiations are conducted using a so-called bilateral "request-offer" process whereby WTO members ask their trading partners to make binding commitments to liberalization in specific areas. To assist their governments in setting priorities, representatives of the financial services industry in the United States, Europe, and other countries are working together—as they did in the negotiations leading to the 1997 agreement—to identify for negotiators key countries for financial services liberalization and specific barriers in each country. (The Doha ministerial declaration called for initial requests to be submitted by June 30, 2002, and offers in response to those requests by March 31, 2003.)

10. As a technical matter, binding existing or ongoing liberalization could involve any of the following actions: removing specific limitations listed in a country's schedule of commitments; binding a mode of supply for which a country had previously entered "unbound"; or listing subsectors or activities that a country had omitted from its schedule. See Key (1997).

11. These measures, which Japan bound in the GATS as so-called "additional commitments," are discussed in chapter 5.

12. In the GATS, countries scheduling commitments in accordance with the Understanding on Commitments in Financial Services committed to a "standstill" under which they may take exceptions to their commitments to market access and national treatment only for existing nonconforming measures. Understanding on Commitments in Financial Services, para. A. See chap. 3, n. 8, regarding the Understanding on Commitments in Financial Services.

13. Specifically, the ratchet in the NAFTA financial services chapter automatically locks in or binds new liberalization with regard to any measure for which a country has taken an exception to an obligation under that chapter. Suppose, for example, a country has taken an exception for an existing nonconforming measure and subsequently amends that measure to provide market access or national treatment. The ratchet locks in the liberalizing amendment—that is, a country is prohibited from reverting to the original nonconforming measure. See North American Free Trade Agreement, art. 1409, para. 1(c).

14. Negotiating guidelines on services adopted in March 2001 by the Council for Trade in Services Special Session state that "[b]ased on multilaterally agreed criteria, account shall be taken and credit shall be given in the negotiations for autonomous liberalization undertaken by Members since previous negotiations." World Trade Organization (2001b), part III. Members were supposed to develop

such criteria before the start of negotiations on specific commitments; as of this writing (January 2003), however, work was still in progress.

15. See Gianviti (1999a, 2000) and International Monetary Fund (2002b). To achieve its own goals, however, the IMF is not precluded from imposing conditionality that may include measures that give effect to obligations undertaken in other international organizations or agreements. For example, if a country had made certain commitments under, say, a World Bank sectoral lending program that were an integral part of the IMF's decision to provide assistance, IMF conditionality might require the country to undertake certain measures that would, in effect, serve to implement its commitments to the World Bank. In the WTO, a ministerial declaration adopted at the close of the Uruguay Round provides that an agreement negotiated in the WTO may not include conditionality vis-à-vis another international institution. See World Trade Organization (1995), Declaration on the Contribution of the World Trade Organization to Achieving Greater Coherence in Global Economic Policymaking, Ministerial Meeting, Trade Negotiations Committee, April 1994, para. 5.

16. In contrast to commitments made in the GATS, IMF conditionality is not permanent, that is, the IMF may impose conditions only for the duration of an IMF program.

17. The letter of intent and economic program that a borrowing country submits to the IMF often contain a broad policy program, only part of which represents IMF conditionality. New guidelines on conditionality approved by the IMF in September 2002 emphasize the need for these documents to distinguish clearly between the conditions on which IMF financial support depends and other elements of the borrowing country's economic program. See International Monetary Fund (2002b).

18. See Korean government (1998). A WTO member may submit a strengthened schedule of commitments at any time. See World Trade Organization (2000d).

19. For example, Korea permits foreign financial firms to provide information and advisory services to Korean residents across borders, but has made no commitments in its GATS financial services schedule for such services in either mode 1 (cross-border services) or mode 2 (consumption abroad).

20. See chap. 3, n. 40. As of this writing (January 2003), no WTO member had yet invoked the balance-of-payments safeguard for services.

21. See Hoekman (1993). For a discussion of an emergency safeguard in relation to financial services as well as principles that should be adhered to if a safeguard provision were to be adopted, see Key (1997), pp. 39–41.

22. See World Trade Organization (1999c).

23. See Key (1997) regarding regulatory barriers versus tariffs.

24. See p. 29 regarding "grandfathering."

25. See Barfield (2001) for an overview of current issues regarding the WTO dispute settlement system. See also Hudec (1999) and Jackson (1997).

26. See chap. 3, n. 8, regarding the Understanding on Commitments in Financial Services.

27. The bound liberalization could involve "phased commitments," that is, commitments that are guaranteed to be implemented by a specified future date that marks the end of a transition period. A government could guarantee that it will lift a restriction by a certain date if it is able to do so by regulation, if it already has any necessary legislative mandate, or if it will be given the authority to do so as part of the approval process for the results of the Doha round negotiations or an accession agreement. See Key (1997). Phased commitments were not used to any significant extent in the 1997 financial services agreement. China, however, in its WTO accession agreement, made a series of phased commitments to market-opening for financial services.

28. The issuance of securities by a corporation is itself *not a* "financial service"; however, the financial services covered by the GATS include many services that are related to the issuance of securities, such as underwriting and distribution.

29. See chapter 2 regarding the treatment of temporary presence of natural persons as a mode of supply in the GATS.

30. See Key (1990, 1997).

31. See GATS, art. II, and Annex on Article II Exemptions. For the extended financial services negotiations, however, special rules applied. As a result, even though the initial schedules of commitments of countries participating in the Uruguay Round negotiations had entered into force on January 1, 1995, members were permitted to submit revised schedules of commitments and lists of MFN exemptions for financial services on two subsequent occasions: during a three-month period that ended on July 28, 1995, for the first set of extended negotiations (which resulted in the so-called interim agreement on financial services); and, for the second set of extended negotiations, during a sixty-day period beginning November 1, 1997. The legal instruments governing the 1995 revisions were the Second Annex on Financial Services, the Decision on Financial Services, and the Decision on the Application of the Second Annex on Financial Services (S/L/6). The 1997 revisions were governed by the Second Decision on Financial Services (S/L/9). These documents are available at http://docsonline.wto.org (accessed January 2003). See also World Trade Organization (1995) for the Second Annex on Financial Services and the Decision on Financial Services.

32. Some WTO members—including some of those that submitted MFN exemptions specifically targeted at financial services—took MFN exemptions for measures applicable to all services sectors that would also be relevant to the financial services sector, including, for example, measures dealing with the temporary presence of natural persons, regulatory frameworks for investment, or real estate ownership. Each member's list of Article II (MFN) exemptions

under the GATS is available at http://docsonline.wto.org (accessed January 2003).

33. In the United States, a policy of reciprocal national treatment for granting primary dealer status was established by the Primary Dealers Act of 1988, § 3502, codified at 22 U.S.C. § 5342 (2000)—that is, primary dealer status is conditional on whether U.S. firms are accorded the "same competitive opportunities" as are available to domestic firms in the foreign country's government debt market. The United States has also taken an MFN exemption for reciprocity policies maintained by various states.

34. An example of this type of MFN exemption taken by an OECD country, in this case, for cross-border services in mode 1, involves Switzerland's requirement that Swiss franc-denominated issues be lead-managed by a bank or securities dealer with a commercial presence in Switzerland. Switzerland listed this requirement as a limitation on market access in its schedule of commitments. Because of its monetary union with Liechtenstein, however, Switzerland has taken an MFN exemption to allow persons established in Liechtenstein to lead-manage such issues without establishing a commercial presence in Switzerland. See chap. 1, n. 12, regarding the criteria for an economic integration agreement.

35. "Dotation" capital requirements imposed by a host country call for the foreign bank to assign a specified amount of capital to the activities of the host-country branch. The term "endowment capital" is often used when the "capital" must be physically held in the host country in domestic currency assets. In the United States and Canada, asset-pledge requirements are used, under which a specified minimum amount of liquid assets such as domestic government securities must be held at a host-country custodian bank. Capital-equivalency requirements should be distinguished from so-called asset-maintenance requirements, which supervisors apply to individual branches experiencing difficulties to ensure that the branch maintains a specified level of eligible assets in excess of liabilities to third parties.

36. For example, the United States has not listed federal or state asset-pledge requirements as limitations in its schedule of commitments. Non-U.S. banks have objected to the economic burden imposed by an across-the-board requirement for their U.S. branches to keep a portion of assets in low-yielding instruments. However, a process of modification of federal and state asset-pledge requirements in the United States is underway. In December 2002, the New York State Banking Department amended its regulations to reduce substantially the asset-pledge requirement and also to cap the pledge for well-rated institutions. Illinois amended its statute, in 1997 and again in 2001, to grant discretionary authority to the state banking commissioner to apply asset-pledge requirements based on a risk-focused assessment of safety and soundness considerations for individual banks. In the 107th U.S. Congress (2001–02), legislation was introduced, but not enacted, that would provide similar discretion to the Comptroller of the Currency

in setting requirements for federally licensed branches; as of this writing (January 2003), the legislation is expected to be reintroduced in the 108th Congress.

37. U.S. Department of the Treasury and Board of Governors of the Federal Reserve System (1992).

38. Although these measures were listed as limitations on market access, they are also limitations to national treatment. The GATS requires measures that are inconsistent with both market access and national treatment to be listed as limitations under market access. See chap. 3, n. 9.

39. This statement appears in a footnote to the so-called headnotes of the EU financial services schedule.

40. See chap. 2, n. 9.

41. More precisely, the limits are applied to branches of non-EEA banks (see chap. 5, n. 32, regarding the European Economic Area).

42. Finance ministry officials also participated in the negotiations. See Exchange of Letters between the Board of Governors of the Federal Reserve System and the Comptroller of the Currency (Richard Spillenkothen, Director, Division of Banking Supervision and Regulation, and Susan F. Krause, Senior Deputy Comptroller for Bank Supervision) and the Bundesaufsichtsamt für das Kreditwesen (Jochen Sanio, Departmental President), February 17, 1994. See also Federal Ministry of Finance [Germany], First Regulation on the exemption of enterprises domiciled outside the European Community from provisions of the German Banking Act, April 21, 1994.

43. See chap. 3, n. 8, regarding the Understanding on Commitments in Financial Services. One OECD country—Switzerland—went further and made broad commitments in mode 1 as well as mode 2. A few OECD countries, however, limited even their commitments for financial information and data processing services and/or advisory services, or made no commitments at all in mode 1. The GATS Annex on Financial Services refers to "advisory, intermediation and other auxiliary financial services" undertaken in connection with any financial service listed in the Annex; examples listed included credit reference and analysis, investment and portfolio research and advice, and advice on acquisitions and corporate restructuring and strategy. With respect to mode 1, however, the Understanding on Commitments in Financial Services covers advisory and other auxiliary financial services but excludes intermediation services.

44. See chap. 4, n. 4, for a list of countries that had acceded to the WTO through full accession negotiations under Article XII of the Marrakesh Agreement Establishing the World Trade Organization as of January 1, 2003.

45. The question of whether such restrictions would be covered by the prudential carve-out or would need to be listed as limitations in a country's schedule of commitments did not arise for countries that scheduled commitments in accordance with the Understanding on Commitments in Financial Services. If a country incorporates the Understanding into its schedule, cross-border financial

services in mode 1 are bound only for financial information and data processing services and advisory services unless other activities are specifically listed.

46. See Mattoo (2000).

47. See chapter 3. The GATS requirement that a member allow capital movements that are an essential part of the cross-border supply of a service mentions only mode 1 (cross-border supply) and not mode 2 (consumption abroad). As a practical matter, however, countries would presumably not have scheduled commitments in either mode 1 or mode 2 unless they were prepared to liberalize any capital transaction that is either an integral part of or closely associated with the provision of the service.

48. See Organization for Economic Cooperation and Development (2000) and Financial Services Authority [UK] (1998). In the United States, for example, SEC regulations provide an exemption that allows foreign broker-dealers to conduct business with broker-dealers in the United States without being subject to U.S. registration requirements. U.S. Securities and Exchange Commission Rule 15a-6. 17 C.F.R. §240 (2002). Also available at www.law.uc.edu/CCL/34ActRls/rule15a-6.html (accessed January 2003).

49. Regulatory authorities in the United Kingdom and the United States were the first to do so. See Financial Services Authority [UK] (1998, 2001a), U.S. Securities and Exchange Commission (1997), and Mann and Carney (2002).

50. Factors listed in IOSCO's *Report on Securities Activities on the Internet* that would support the assertion of regulatory authority by a host country include: (a) "targeting" host-country customers; (b) accepting orders from or providing services to them; and (c) using e-mail or other media to "push" information to them. International Organization of Securities Commissions (1998). See also International Organization of Securities Commissions (2001) and Mann and Carney (2002).

51. Suppose that despite negotiators' efforts, a host country continues to refuse to provide, even in practice, national treatment and market access for some or all cross-border financial services. In that event, an immediate short-run objective is ensuring that the country provides national treatment and market access—and makes the appropriate binding commitments—to enable the services to be provided to host-country residents through establishment of a commercial presence. This would need to be accomplished, however, without prejudice to the goal of liberalization of cross-border services.

Chapter 5: Nondiscriminatory Structural Barriers

1. See the discussion of cross-border services in chapter 4 regarding the issue of binding exemptions from prudential measures that provide national treatment and market access in the first place.

2. In 2001, both the United States and Canada submitted proposals on over-all regulatory transparency for the GATS negotiations in the Doha round. See World Trade Organization (2001d, 2001f). The United States had previously submitted, as an attachment to its initial sectoral proposal for financial services, "some initial views" on transparency and other principles for regulation of financial services. World Trade Organization (2000a).

3. See Roberts (1999), Martin and Feldman (1998), Florini (2000), Iida and Nielson (2001), Thompson and Iida (2001), International Monetary Fund (1999), and Group of 22 (G-22) Working Group on Transparency and Account-ability (1998). The G-22, an ad hoc group established in 1997, included the G-7 countries, other major industrial countries, and a number of emerging market economies. See International Monetary Fund (2002a).

4. Thompson and Iida (2001).

5. See 5 U.S.C. § 553 (2000). Also available at www4.law.cornell.edu/uscode/5/553.html (accessed January 2003).

6. GATS, art. III, para. 1.

7. Article VI of the GATS (Domestic Regulation) already includes a require-ment for providing information about the status of an application but only for services for which a specific commitment to national treatment and market access has been made. See GATS, art. VI, para. 3, and chapter 3.

8. See GATS, art. VI, paras. 1 and 3.

9. See GATS, art. VI, para. 2.

10. International Organization of Securities Commissions (2002).

11. As discussed in chapter 3, Article VI contains a mandate for further work on standards and licensing requirements. See GATS, art. VI, para. 4.

12. See Financial Stability Forum (2002a, 2002b).

13. International Organization of Securities Commissions (2002), Principle 4 and explanatory text. The explanation also states that, in the formation of policy, regulators "should have a process for consultation with the public including those who may be affected by the policy; disclose publicly policies in important oper-ational areas; observe standards of procedural fairness; [and] have regard for the cost of compliance with the regulation." The issue of regulatory transparency is not addressed by the Basel Core Principles for Effective Banking Supervision.

14. International Monetary Fund (1999), Principle 6.4. See also International Monetary Fund (2000).

15. International Organization of Securities Commissions (2002) and Basel Committee on Banking Supervision (1997).

16. "Effective market access" is an undefined term that has been used in ambiguous and contradictory ways in the context of international trade in finan-cial services. For example, it has been used broadly to encompass all second-pillar barriers and also, much more narrowly, to refer to de facto national treatment. See Key (1990). In this study, however, "effective market access"

involves only those second-pillar barriers that, in practice, keep foreign firms from competing in host-country markets.

17. Japan also made significant additional commitments for insurance services with regard to barriers involving limitations on lines of business and lack of transparency. In addition, one insurance commitment was actually aimed at maintaining for a certain period of time a restriction on new entrants into a niche market, the so-called third sector of accident, medical, and nursing care insurance. The purpose was to protect the interests of foreign firms in this market until they could enter and compete with domestic firms in other market segments. See Japan–United States Measures Regarding Financial Services (1995), Japan–United States Measures Regarding Insurance (1994), and Japan–United States Supplementary Measures Regarding Insurance (1996).

18. See World Trade Organization (2001a) for a comprehensive discussion of the distinction between quantitative measures, particularly economic needs tests, listed in Article XVI of the GATS (Market Access) and domestic regulatory measures.

19. See Pozen (2002).

20. In the GATS, additional commitments are scheduled as so-called positive lists of liberalizing measures that reduce or remove existing barriers. A country would, of course, be unwilling to make a commitment to liberalize with respect to a measure that it regards as prudential. A country might need to rely on the prudential carve-out, however, if circumstances were to change such that it decided to reintroduce for prudential reasons a measure that was inconsistent with its additional commitments.

21. See chapter 3 and Investment Company Institute (2001).

22. Under such principles, mutual funds must maintain portfolios that comply with their stated investment objectives, disclose portfolio holdings periodically, maintain sufficient portfolio liquidity to meet redemptions, and keep fund assets safeguarded. Pension funds must act solely in the interests of the pension plan and its participants, make investments in accordance with principles of diversification and prudence, and safeguard plan assets. See, for example, International Organization of Securities Commissions (1994) regarding collective investment schemes, and European Commission (2000) and De Ryck (1999) regarding pension funds.

23. The Gramm-Leach-Bliley Act of 1999 eliminated the nondiscriminatory structural barriers that prevented affiliations between banks and insurance firms and affiliations between banks and companies that are principally engaged in securities underwriting and dealing activities—beyond certain government securities underwriting activities. These barriers were deeply rooted in the U.S. political structure, and their impact on foreign financial firms was not a factor in the failure of many previous efforts to remove them. Consistent with U.S. commitments in the GATS, the legislation provides national treatment for foreign financial firms. See Gramm-Leach-Bliley Act of 1999, Pub.L. No. 106-102, 113

Stat. 1338 (1999), and Federal Reserve System—Bank Holding Companies and Change in Bank Control (Regulation Y), 12 C.F.R. § 225.81-225.94 (2002). See also Meyer (2001a) and Olson (2002).

24. GATS, art. VI, para. 4.

25. Although some countries accord, in effect, unilateral recognition to the regulation and supervision of mutual funds registered in certain jurisdictions by allowing the funds to be sold across borders to domestic residents, tax barriers may make such funds unattractive to domestic residents. For example, mutual funds registered in the United States were not marketed to Australian residents until Australia accorded, in effect, unilateral recognition of U.S. tax law with respect to required distributions from mutual funds. Specifically, on the basis of a determination that U.S. requirements for taxable distributions are similar to those of Australia, Australia allowed U.S. mutual funds to be purchased by Australian residents without applying its rules for imputing tax on earnings from foreign mutual funds marketed in Australia (see chap. 2, n. 14). The U.S.-Canada multijurisdictional disclosure system (MJDS) is designed to facilitate the cross-border issuance of securities by U.S. and Canadian companies by recognizing disclosure standards of the issuer's home country. Issuers of securities, however, are not financial service providers under the GATS. In the insurance sector, Switzerland is a party to two mutual recognition agreements (see chap. 5, n. 29).

26. Specifically, the GATS provides that if WTO members negotiate a recognition arrangement or agreement, they must provide other WTO members the opportunity to negotiate their accession to such an arrangement or agreement or to negotiate a similar arrangement or agreement. If a WTO member unilaterally recognizes the prudential measures of another country, it must permit any WTO member to demonstrate that its measures should also be recognized. See GATS, Annex on Financial Services, para. 3.

27. In contrast to Article VII, however, the recognition provision in the Annex on Financial Services does not contain a requirement for prior notification to the Council on Trade in Services.

28. See chap. 4, n. 42.

29. In the insurance sector, two mutual recognition agreements to which Switzerland is a party are based on harmonization to EU standards. The 1989 insurance agreement between Switzerland and the European Community (which covers non-life insurance provided through branches) is based on Switzerland's conforming its prudential regulations, primarily with regard to solvency requirements, to the standards set forth in EU directives. The 1996 Switzerland-Liechtenstein insurance agreement, which, in effect, treats Switzerland as if it were a member of the EEA (see chap. 5, n. 32) but only vis-à-vis Liechtenstein and only in the insurance sector, was facilitated by the previous Swiss harmonization of prudential rules to EU standards and by the fact that Liechtenstein, to

become a member of the EEA, had been required to adopt the *acquis communau-taire* and agree to conform to future EU legislation.

30. For example, determination of a foreign bank's capital adequacy as part of a host-country licensing process could be speeded up by recognition of the home country's implementation of the Basel risk-based capital standards (see chap. 3, n. 45). Such recognition could allow the use of capital ratios calculated for home-country supervisory purposes, thereby avoiding the process of recalculating the ratios under host-country rules. The ratios would, however, still need to meet host-country capital standards, which might be higher than those of the home country.

31. International Banking Act of 1978, § 7(d), codified as amended at 12 U.S.C. § 3105(d) (2000). Also available at www4.law.cornell.edu/uscode/12/3105.html (accessed January 2003). This requirement is often referred to as "comprehensive consolidated supervision." See Federal Reserve System—International Banking Operations (Regulation K), 12 C.F.R. § 211.24 (2002).

32. The European Economic Area comprises the fifteen EU member states and three members of the European Free Trade Association (EFTA)—namely, Norway, Iceland, and Liechtenstein. Switzerland, the fourth member of the EFTA, is not a party to the EEA Agreement. Like financial firms incorporated in EU member states, financial firms incorporated in the EFTA states that are members of the EEA may also operate throughout the EEA on the basis of a "single license." The EEA agreement entered into force on January 1, 1994. See http://secretariat.efta.int/euroeco/ (accessed January 2003).

33. See chap. 3, n. 53, regarding bank supervision and the European Central Bank.

34. A precondition established by the Court of Justice is the absence of prior Community harmonization in the area. Additional conditions include nonduplication, that is, the interest is not already protected by the home member state; necessity, that is, whether the measure is necessary for the stated objective; and proportionality, that is, whether there is a less restrictive means of achieving the same objective. See European Commission (1997). The general good exception is very different from the GATS prudential carve-out. First, in the context of the intra-EU home-country approach, the general good exception is designed to allow host countries to impose their own rules on a national treatment basis; the prudential carve-out applies in the context of host-country rules and, *inter alia,* allows host countries to apply those rules on a less-than-national-treatment basis. Second, the general good exception is much broader in scope than the prudential carve-out, which applies only to prudential measures. Third, the general good exception is subject to the strict criteria described above; by contrast, the prudential carve-out is not subject to any restrictions other than the antiabuse provision.

35. Most EU single-market legislation is in the form of directives. Each directive specifies a date by which the member states must conform their national laws or

regulations to the provisions of the directive; typically the states have two years to do so.

36. The euro was introduced as a legal currency on January 1, 1999, and the eleven currencies of the participating member states became subdivisions of the euro. Euro banknotes and coins were introduced on January 1, 2002. As of January 2003, the "Eurozone" comprised twelve of the fifteen EU member states, namely, Austria, Belgium, Finland, France, Germany, Greece (which joined in January 2001), Ireland, Italy, Luxembourg, the Netherlands, Portugal, and Spain.

37. See Presidency Conclusions of the respective European Councils at http://ue.eu.int/en/Info/eurocouncil/index.htm (accessed January 2003).

38. See European Commission (1999). In February 2001, the so-called Lamfalussy report proposed a framework, endorsed by the Stockholm European Council in March 2001, to improve and streamline the EU legislative process for rules dealing with securities markets to keep pace with rapidly changing market developments. See Committee of Wise Men on the Regulation of European Securities Markets (2001).

39. In general, remaining intra-EU barriers to the cross-border provision of retail financial services under the single license are much stronger than those for provision of retail services through branches. Because of technological developments, however, use of the single license for EU-wide branching to provide retail banking services may now be less likely to occur.

40. To deal with those concerns in relation to selling contracts to consumers— within or across national borders—for credit cards, investment funds, or pension plans via telephone, fax, or the Internet, the Distance Marketing Directive (DMD) for financial services, which was adopted in September 2002, relies in some areas on the approach of full harmonization, that is, establishment of uniform consumer protection measures from which member states may not deviate. Moreover, the European Commission's November 2002 proposal for a new directive on Investment Services and Regulated Markets—one of the most important pieces of legislation under the Financial Services Action Plan—includes more extensive harmonization of rules as compared with the current Investment Services Directive (ISD) in order to ensure, *inter alia,* an adequate level of investor protection, especially for retail investors. See http://europa.eu.int/eur-lex/pri/en/oj/dat/2002/l_271 /l_27120021009en00160024.pdf and www.europa.eu.int/eur-lex/en/com/pdf/ 2002/com2002_0625en01.pdf (accessed January 2003).

41. Most financial services legislation is enacted under the "co-decision procedure," which involves adoption of directives by the Council—in this case, usually the Council of Economic and Finance Ministers, known as the ECOFIN Council— using "qualified majority voting" (i.e., weighted majority voting) and by the European Parliament, which, under the co-decision procedure has the power to veto legislation. A member state is obligated to transpose a directive into national law within a prescribed period of time and ensure enforcement, even if

the member state opposed the directive during the Community legislative process. Community law is accepted by the member states as prevailing over national law and also over national constitutions, and judgments and rulings of the Court of Justice of the European Communities are binding in the member states. Although the principle of supremacy of Community law is not explicitly stated in the EC Treaty, the supremacy of both the treaty and secondary legislation, such as directives, has been confirmed in the case law of the Court of Justice. See chap. 3, n. 19, regarding the distinction between the "European Community" and the "European Union," and chap. 3, n. 53, regarding the European Central Bank and banking supervision.

42. The so-called Codified Banking Directive (Directive 2000/12/EC of the European Parliament and of the Council of 20 March 2000 relating to the taking up and pursuit of the business of credit institutions), enacted in 2000, replaced, without substantive changes, the Second Banking Directive and a number of other EU banking directives, together with all of the amendments to the directives. See http://europa.eu.int/eur-lex/en/consleg/main/2000/en_2000L0012_index.html (accessed January 2003).

43. For banking legislation in force see www.europa.eu.int/eur-lex/en/lif/reg/en_register_06202020.html (accessed January 2003). For securities markets and investment services, see www.europa.eu.int/eur-lex/en/lif/reg/en_register_06202025.html (accessed January 2003).

References

Barfield, Claude 2001. *Free Trade, Sovereignty, Democracy: The Future of the World Trade Organization*. Washington, D.C.: AEI Press.

Basel Committee on Banking Supervision. 1997. *Core Principles for Effective Banking Supervision*. Basel Committee Publications 30. Basel: Bank for International Settlements. September. Available at www.bis.org/publ/bcbs30a.pdf (accessed January 2003).

———. 1999. *Core Principles Methodology*. Basel Committee Publications 61. Basel: Bank for International Settlements. October. Available at www.bis.org/publ/bcbs61.pdf (accessed January 2003).

———. 2000. "Cross-Border Electronic Banking Issues for Bank Supervisors." In *Electronic Banking Group Initiatives and White Papers*. Basel: Bank for International Settlements. September. Available at www.bis.org/publ/bcbs76.pdf (accessed January 2003).

———. 2001. *Conducting a Supervisory Self-Assessment: Practical Application*. Basel Committee Publications 81. Basel: Bank for International Settlements. April. Available at www.bis.org/publ/bcbs81.pdf (accessed January 2003).

Beviglia Zampetti, Americo, and Pierre Sauvé. 1996. "Onwards to Singapore: The International Contestability of Markets and the New Trade Agenda." *The World Economy* 7 (2): 133–43.

British Invisibles. 1998. *Opening Markets for Financial Services: The BI Guide to the Financial Services Agreement in the World Trade Organization*. London: British Invisibles [effective February 1, 2001, International Financial Services, London].

Claessens, Stijn, Asli Dermirgüç-Kunt, and Harry Huizinga. 1998. "How Does Foreign Entry Affect the Domestic Banking Market?" Policy Research Working Paper 1918. Washington, D.C.: World Bank.

Claessens, Stijn, Simeon Djankov, and Daniela Klingebiel. 1999. "Financial Restructuring in East Asia: Halfway There?" Financial Sector Discussion Paper 3. Washington, D.C.: World Bank.

Claessens, Stijn, and Thomas Glaessner. 1997. "Internationalization of Financial Services in East Asia." Paper presented at Conference on Investment Liberalization and Financial Reform in the Asia-Pacific Region, Sydney, Australia, August 29–31.

Claessens, Stijn, Thomas Glaessner, and Daniela Klingebiel. 2000. "Electronic Finance: Reshaping the Financial Landscape around the World." Financial Sector Discussion Paper 4. Washington, D.C.: World Bank.

———. 2001. "E-finance in Emerging Markets: Is Leapfrogging Possible?" Financial Sector Discussion Paper 7. Washington, D.C.: World Bank.

Clarke, George R.G., Robert Cull, and Maria Soledad Martinez Peria. 2001. "Does Foreign Bank Penetration Reduce Access to Credit in Developing Countries?" Policy Research Working Paper 2716. Washington, D.C.: World Bank.

Clifford Chance. 1997. *The EU Investment Services Directive: The Impact on Cross-Border Business.* London: Clifford Chance.

Committee of Wise Men on the Regulation of European Securities Markets. 2001. Final Report [known as Lamfalussy Report]. Available at www.europa.eu.int/comm/internal_market/en/finances/general/lamfalussyen.pdf (accessed January 2003).

Conthe, Manuel, and Stefan Ingves. 2001. "Financial Sector Assessment Program." Commentary. Washington, D.C.: International Monetary Fund. March 9. Available at www.imf.org/external/np/vc/2001/030901.htm (accessed January 2003).

De Ryck, Koen. 1996. *European Pension Funds: Their Impact on European Capital Markets and Competitiveness.* Brussels: European Federation for Retirement Provision. Available at www.efrp.org/downloads/efrp_publications/1996report.pdf (accessed January 2003).

———. 1999. *Rebuilding Pensions: Security, Efficiency, Affordability.* Brussels: European Commission. Available at www.europa.eu.int/comm/internal_market/pensions/docs/studies/1999-occupa-full_en.pdf (accessed January 2003).

DeYoung, Robert. 2001. "The Internet's Place in the Banking Industry." *Chicago Fed Letter* 163. Chicago: Federal Reserve Bank of Chicago.

Dobson, Wendy, and Gary Clyde Hufbauer. 2001. *World Capital Markets: Challenge to the G-10.* Washington, D.C.: Institute for International Economics.

Dobson, Wendy, and Pierre Jacquet. 1998. *Financial Services Liberalization in the WTO.* Washington, D.C.: Institute for International Economics.

Eichengreen, Barry, and Michael Mussa, with Giovanni Dell'Ariccia, Enrica Detragiache, Gian Maria Milesi-Ferretti, and Andrew Tweedie. 1998. "Capital Account Liberalization: Theoretical and Practical Aspects." Occasional Paper 172. Washington, D.C.: International Monetary Fund.

European Commission. 1997. *Freedom to Provide Services and the Interest of the General Good in the Second Banking Directive.* Interpretive Communication. SEC(97) 1193 final. Brussels: Commission of the European Communities. June 20. Available at www.europa.eu.int/comm/internal_market/en/finances/banks/bank1en.pdf (accessed January 2003).

———. 1999. *Implementing the Framework for Financial Markets: Action Plan.* Communication. COM(1999) 232. Brussels: Commission of the European

Communities. May 11. Available at www.europa.eu.int/comm/internal_market/en/finances/general/actionen.pdf (accessed January 2003).

———. 2000. *Proposal for a Directive of the European Parliament and of the Council on the Activities of Institutions for Occupational Retirement Provision.* COM (2000) 507 final. Brussels: Commission of the European Communities. October 11. Available at www.efrp.org/downloads/eu_publications/10october2000.pdf (accessed January 2003).

———. 2002. *Financial Services: An Improving Climate—But Quite Some Way to Go.* Sixth Progress Report on the Financial Services Action Plan. COM (2002) 267. Brussels: Commission of the European Communities. June 3. Available at www.europa.eu.int/comm/internal_market/en/finances/actionplan/progress6_en.pdf (accessed January 2003).

European Services Forum. 2001. "Domestic Regulation: Preliminary Discussion Paper." Brussels: European Services Forum. June 5. Available at www.esf.be/f_e_docs.htm#top (accessed January 2003).

Financial Leaders Group. 2001. "Commentary on Proposals for Liberalisation in Financial Services." September 21. Available at www.uscsi.org/publications/papers/FLG%20Commentary%20Sept%202001.pdf (accessed January 2003).

Financial Services Authority. 1998. Treatment of Material on Overseas Internet World Wide Web Sites Accessible in the UK but Not Intended for Investors in the UK. Guidance 2/98. Available at www.fsa.gov.uk/pubs/guidance/gr02_1998.pdf (accessed January 2003).

———. 2001a. *The FSA's Approach to the Regulation of E-Commerce.* Discussion Paper 6. Available at www.fsa.gov.uk/pubs/discussion/dp6.pdf (accessed January 2003).

———. 2001b. *Wholesale-Only Deposit-Takers.* Consultation Paper 88. Available at www.fsa.gov.uk/pubs/cp/cp88.pdf (accessed January 2003).

Financial Stability Forum. 2002a. *Compendium of Standards.* Available at www.fsforum.org/compendium/about.html (accessed January 2003).

———. 2002b. *Ongoing and Recent Work Relevant to Sound Financial Systems.* Semiannual status report (September). Available at www.fsforum.org/publications/Ongoing0902.pdf (accessed January 2003).

Findlay, Christopher, and Tony Warren. 2000. Introduction to *Impediments to Trade in Services: Measurement and Policy Implications,* edited by Christopher Findlay and Tony Warren. London and New York: Routledge.

Fischer, Stanley. 2000. "The IMF and the Financial Sector." Presentation. Seminar on Financial Risks, System Stability, and Economic Globalization. Washington, D.C.: International Monetary Fund. June 5.

Fischer, Stanley, Richard N. Cooper, Rudiger Dornbusch, Peter M. Garber, Carlos Massad, Jacques J. Polak, Dani Rodrik, and Savak S. Tarapore. 1998. *Should the IMF Pursue Capital-Account Convertibility?* Essays in International Finance 207. Princeton, N.J.: Princeton University Press.

Florini, Ann M. 2000. "Does the Invisible Hand Need a Transparent Glove? The Politics of Transparency." In *Annual World Bank Conference on Development Economics 1999,* edited by Boris Pleskovic and Joseph E. Stiglitz, 163–84. Washington, D.C.: World Bank.

Freiberg, Kenneth. 1996. "Introductory Note—World Trade Organization: Second Protocol to the General Agreement on Trade in Services (GATS) and Related Decisions." *International Legal Materials* 35: 199–202.

Furst, Karen, William W. Lang, and Daniel E. Nolle. 2000. "Internet Banking in the U.S.: Landscape, Prospects, Industry Implications." *Journal of Financial Transformation* 2: 46–52.

Gianviti, Francois. 1999a. "Decision Making in the International Monetary Fund." In International Monetary Fund, *Current Developments in Monetary and Financial Law.* Vol. 1. Washington, D.C.: International Monetary Fund.

———. 1999b. "The International Monetary Fund and the Liberalization of Capital Movements." In International Monetary Fund, *Current Developments in Monetary and Financial Law.* Vol. 1. Washington, D.C.: International Monetary Fund.

———. 2000. "The Reform of the International Monetary Fund (Conditionality and Surveillance)." *The International Lawyer* 34: 107–16.

"Going for Brokers: Online Stockbroking Is One of the Internet's Big Success Stories." 2000. *The Economist,* May 18.

Graham, Edward M., and Robert Z. Lawrence. 1996. "Measuring the International Contestability of Markets: A Conceptual Approach." *Journal of World Trade* 30 (5): 5–20.

Greenspan, Alan. 1998. "International Economic and Financial Systems." Testimony before the Committee on Banking and Financial Services, U.S. House of Representatives. September 16.

Group of 22 (G-22). 1998. *Report of the Working Group on Transparency and Accountability.* Available at www.bis.org/publ/othp01b.pdf and www.imf.org/external/np/g22/taarep.pdf (accessed January 2003).

Hagan, Sean L. 1999. "The Design of the International Monetary Fund's Jurisdiction over Capital Movements." In International Monetary Fund, *Current Developments in Monetary and Financial Law.* Vol. 1. Washington, D.C.: International Monetary Fund.

Hawkins, John, and Dubravko Mihaljek. 2001. "The Banking Industry in the Emerging Market Economies: Competition, Consolidation, and Systemic Stability: An Overview." In *The Banking Industry in the Emerging Market Economies: Competition, Consolidation, and Systemic Stability.* BIS Papers 4. Basel: Bank for International Settlements.

Hilton, Andrew. 2000. "Internet Banking: A Fragile Flower." Discussion Paper 44. London: Centre for the Study of Financial Innovation.

Hoekman, Bernard M. 1993. "Safeguard Provisions and International Trade Agreements Involving Services." *The World Economy* 16 (1): 29–49.

———. 1996. "Assessing the General Agreement on Trade in Services." In *The Uruguay Round and the Developing Countries,* edited by Will Martin and L. Alan Winters. Cambridge: Cambridge University Press.

———. 1997. "Competition Policy and the Global Trading System." *The World Economy* 20 (4): 383–406.

———. 2000. "Towards a More Balanced and Comprehensive Services Agreement." In *The WTO after Seattle,* edited by Jeffrey J. Schott. Washington, D.C.: Institute for International Economics.

Hoekman, Bernard M., Patrick Low, and Petros C. Mavroidis. 1996. "Regulation, Competition Policy, and Market Access Negotiations: Lessons from the Telecommunications Sector." In *Competition Policy for an Integrated Global Economy,* edited by Einar Hope. London: Routledge.

Hoekman, Bernard M., and Petros C. Mavroidis, eds. 1997. *Law and Policy in Public Purchasing: The WTO Agreement on Government Procurement.* Ann Arbor: University of Michigan Press.

———. 1999. "WTO Dispute Settlement, Transparency, and Surveillance." *The World Economy* 23 (4): 527–42.

Hoekman, Bernard, and Patrick A. Messerlin. 2000. "Liberalizing Trade in Services: Reciprocal Negotiations and Regulatory Reform." In *GATS 2000: New Directions in Services Trade Liberalization,* edited by Pierre Sauvé and Robert M. Stern. Washington, D.C.: Brookings Institution Press.

Hoekman, Bernard, and Pierre Sauvé. 1994. "Liberalizing Trade in Services." Discussion Paper 343. Washington, D.C.: World Bank.

Holder, William E. 1999. "Fund Jurisdiction over Capital Movements." Comments, Panel on Preventing Asian-Type Crises: Who, If Anyone, Should Have Jurisdiction over Capital Movements? *ILSA Journal of International and Comparative Law* 5 (2): 407–15.

Houpt, James V. 1999. "International Activities of U.S. Banks and in U.S. Banking Markets." *Federal Reserve Bulletin* 85 (September): 599–615.

Hudec, Robert E. 1999. "The New WTO Dispute Settlement Procedures: An Overview of the First Three Years." *Minnesota Journal of Global Trade* 8 (1): 1–53.

Iida, Keiya, and Julia Nielson. 2001. "Transparency in Domestic Regulation: Prior Consultation." In *Trade in Services: Negotiating Issues and Approaches,* edited by Julia Nielson and Pierre Sauvé Paris: Organization for Economic Cooperation and Development.

International Monetary Fund. 1993. *Balance-of-Payments Manual.* 5th ed. Washington, D.C.: International Monetary Fund.

———. 1999. *Code of Good Practices on Transparency in Monetary and Financial Policies: Declaration of Principles.* Washington, D.C.: International Monetary Fund. Available at www.imf.org/external/np/mae/mft/code/eng/code2e.pdf (accessed January 2003).

————. 2000. Supporting Document to the *Code of Good Practices on Transparency in Monetary and Financial Policies*. Washington, D.C.: International Monetary Fund. Available at www.imf.org/external/np/mae/mft/sup/index.htm (accessed January 2003).

————. 2001a. "IMF Reviews Strengthening Country Ownership of Fund-Supported Programs." Public Information Notice (PIN) 01/125. December 14. Available at www.imf.org/external/np/sec/pn/2001/PN01125.HTM (accessed January 2003)

————. 2001b. *Reforming the International Financial Architecture: Progress through 2000*. IMF Issues Brief. Available at www.imf.org/external/np/exr/ib/2001/030901.htm (accessed January 2003).

————. 2001c. *Strengthening Country Ownership of Fund-Supported Programs*. Policy Development and Review Department. December. Available at www.imf.org/external/np/pdr/cond/2001/eng/strength/120501.htm (accessed January 2003).

————. 2002a. "A Brief Guide to Committees, Groups, and Clubs: A Factsheet." September. Available at www.imf.org/external/np/exr/facts/groups.htm (accessed January 2003).

————. 2002b. *Guidelines on Conditionality*. September 25. Available at www.imf.org/External/np/pdr/cond/2002/eng/guid/092302.pdf (accessed January 2003).

————. 2002c. "International Trade in Services: Recent Methodological Developments." Available at www.imf.org/external/np/sta/itserv/methdev.htm (accessed January 2003).

————. 2002d. "Standards and Codes." Available at www.imf.org/external/standards/index.htm (accessed January 2003).

International Organization of Securities Commissions. 1994. *Report on Investment Management—Principles for the Regulation of Collective Investment Schemes and Explanatory Memorandum*. Technical Committee. October. Madrid: International Organization of Securities Commissions.

————. 1998. *Report on Securities Activities on the Internet*. Technical Committee. Internet Task Force. September. Available at www.iosco.org/pubdocs/pdf/IOSCOPD83.pdf (accessed January 2003).

————. 2001. *Report on Securities Activities on the Internet II*. Technical Committee. Internet Task Force. June. Available at www.iosco.org/pubdocs/pdf/IOSCOPD120.pdf (accessed January 2003).

————. 2002. *Objectives and Principles of Securities Regulation* (updated with references to work done by IOSCO since September 1998). February. Available at www.iosco.org/pubdocs/pdf/IOSCOPD125.pdf (accessed January 2003).

Investment Company Institute. 1999. "Regulatory Approaches to the Internet: Fund Marketing and Privacy Act." Presentation at 13th Annual International Investment Funds Conference, South Africa. Washington, D.C.: Investment Company Institute.

———. 2001. "Asset Management." Presentation at Financial Services Seminar. Council for Trade in Services. The World Trade Organization, Geneva. October 11. Washington, D.C.: Investment Company Institute.

Ishii, Shogo, and Karl F. Habermeier. 2002. *Capital Account Liberalization and Financial Sector Stability—Considerations for Sequencing.* Occasional Paper 211. Washington, D.C.: International Monetary Fund.

Jackson, John H. 1997. *The World Trading System: Law and Policy of International Economic Relations.* 2d ed. Cambridge, Mass.: MIT Press.

Japan–United States Measures Regarding Financial Services. February 13, 1995. *International Legal Materials* 34: 617–60. Also available at www.mac.doc.gov/ japan/source/menu/miscellaneous/servi.html (accessed January 2003).

Japan–United States Measures Regarding Insurance. October 11, 1994. *International Legal Materials* 34: 661-75. Also available at www.mac.doc.gov/ japan/source/menu/insurance/insurejp.html (accessed January 2003).

Japan–United States Supplementary Measures Regarding Insurance. December 24, 1996. Available at www.mac.doc.gov/japan/source/menu/insurance/ supjpn.html (accessed January 2003).

Kampf, Roger. 1995. "A Step in the Right Direction: The Interim Deal on Financial Services in the GATS." *International Trade Law and Regulation* 1 (5): 157–66.

———. 1998. "Financial Services in the WTO: Third Time Lucky." *International Trade Law and Regulation* 4 (3): 111–23.

Karsenty, Guy. 2000. "Assessing Trade in Services by Mode of Supply." In *GATS 2000: New Directions in Services Trade Liberalization,* edited by Pierre Sauvé and Robert M. Stern. Washington, D.C.: Brookings Institution Press.

Key, Sydney J. 1989a. "Financial Integration in the European Community." *International Finance Discussion Papers* 349 (April). Washington, D.C.: Board of Governors of the Federal Reserve System.

———. 1989b. "Mutual Recognition: Integration of the Financial Sector in the European Community." *Federal Reserve Bulletin* 75 (September): 591–609.

———. 1990. "Is National Treatment Still Viable? U.S. Policy in Theory and Practice." *Journal of International Banking Law* 5 (9): 365–81.

———. 1994. "Deposit-Guarantee Directive." In *Banking and EC Law: Commentary,* edited by Martijn van Empel and René Smits. Amsterdam Financial Series. Deventer, The Netherlands: Kluwer Law and Taxation Publishers.

———. 1997. *Financial Services in the Uruguay Round and the WTO.* Occasional Papers 54. Washington, D.C.: Group of Thirty.

———. 1999. "Trade Liberalization and Prudential Regulation: The International Framework for Financial Services." *International Affairs* 75 (1): 61–75.

Key, Sydney J., and Hal S. Scott. 1991. *International Trade in Banking Services: A Conceptual Framework.* Occasional Papers 35. Washington, D.C.: Group of Thirty.

Kono, Masamichi, and Ludger Schuknecht. 1998. "Financial Services Trade, Capital Flows, and Financial Stability." Staff Working Paper ERAD-98-12. Geneva: World Trade Organization.

Kono, Masamichi, Patrick Low, Mukela Luanga, Aaditya Mattoo, Maika Oshikawa, and Ludger Schuknecht. 1997. *Opening Markets in Financial Services and the Role of the GATS.* Geneva: World Trade Organization.

Korean government. 1998. Letter of Intent, with Memorandum on the Economic Program, submitted to the International Monetary Fund. February 7. Available at www.imf.org/external/np/loi/020798.htm (accessed January 2003).

Krugman, Paul. 1998. "Saving Asia: It's Time to Get Radical." *Fortune,* September 7.

Lane, Timothy, Atish Ghosh, Javier Hamann, Steven Phillips, Mariannce Schulze-Ghattas, and Tsidi Tsikata. 1999. *IMF-Supported Programs in Indonesia, Korea, and Thailand: A Preliminary Assessment.* Occasional Paper 178. Washington, D.C.: International Monetary Fund.

Lawrence, Robert Z. 1996. "Toward Globally Contestable Markets." In *Organization for Economic Cooperation and Development, Market Access after the Uruguay Round: Investment, Competition, and Technology Perspectives.* Paris: Organization for Economic Cooperation and Development.

Leckow, Ross. B. 2000. "The Role of the International Monetary Fund in the Liberalization of Capital Movements." *Wisconsin International Law Journal* 17 (3): 515–26.

Levine, Ross. 1996. "Foreign Banks, Financial Development, and Economic Growth." In *Harmonization versus Competition: International Financial Markets,* edited by Claude Barfield. Washington, D.C.: AEI Press.

Low, Patrick, and Aaditya Mattoo. 2000. "Is There a Better Way? Alternative Approaches to Liberalization under the GATS." In *GATS 2000: New Directions in Services Trade Liberalization,* edited by Pierre Sauvé and Robert M. Stern. Washington, D.C.: Brookings Institution Press.

Mann, Michael D., and Eva Marie Carney. 2002. "Jurisdiction in Cyberspace: International Implications of Electronic Markets." In *Securities in the Electronic Age: A Practical Guide to the Law and Regulation,* edited by John F. Olson and Carmen J. Lawrence. 3d ed. Little Falls, N.J.: Glasser LegalWorks.

Martin, Robert, and Estelle Feldman. 1998. "Access to Information in Developing Countries." Working Paper. Transparency International. Available at www.transparency.org/working_papers/martin-feldman/index.html (accessed January 2003).

Mattoo, Aaditya. 1997. "National Treatment in the GATS—Cornerstone or Pandora's Box?" *Journal of World Trade* 31 (1): 107–35.

———. 1999. "MFN and the GATS." In *Regulatory Barriers and the Principle of Non-discrimination in World Trade Law: Past, Present, and Future.* Vol. 2 of *The World Trade Forum,* edited by Thomas Cottier and Petros C. Mavroidis. Ann Arbor: University of Michigan Press.

————.2000. "Financial Services and the WTO: Liberalization Commitments of Developing and Transition Economies." *The World Economy* 23 (3): 351–86.

Mattoo, Aaditya, Randeep Rathindran, and Arvind Subramanian. 2001. "Measuring Services Trade Liberalization and Its Impact on Economic Growth: An Illustration." *World Bank Working Paper* 2655. Washington, D.C.: World Bank.

Mattoo, Aaditya, and Ludger Schuknecht. 2000. "Trade Policies for Electronic Commerce." *Policy Research Working Paper* 2380. Washington, D.C.: World Bank.

McGuire, Greg, and Michael Schuele. 2000. "Restrictiveness of International Trade in Banking Services." In *Impediments to Trade in Services: Measurement and Policy Implications,* edited by Christopher Findlay and Tony Warren. London and New York: Routledge.

McKenzie, Duncan. 2002. "Impact of Liberalising Financial Services." *IFSL Brief.* London: International Financial Services, London. Available at www.ifsl. org.uk/uploads/RP_Liberal_of_fin_serv_12_01.pdf (accessed January 2003).

Meyer, Laurence H. 2001a. "Implementing the Gramm-Leach-Bliley Act: One Year Later." Remarks before the American Law Institute and American Bar Association, Washington, D.C. February 15.

————. 2001b. "Financial Stability in Emerging Markets: What Have We Accomplished and What Remains to Be Done?" Remarks at the Center for Strategic and International Studies, Washington, D.C. December 18.

Morris, Rosemary. 2001. "Scheduling of Economic Needs Tests in the GATS: An Overview." In *Trade in Services: Negotiating Issues and Approaches,* edited by Julia Nielson and Pierre Sauvé Paris: Organization for Economic Cooperation and Development.

Nieto, Maria J. 2001. "Reflections on the Regulatory Approach to E-Finance." In *Electronic Finance: A New Perspective and Challenges.* BIS Papers 7. Basel: Bank for International Settlements.

North American Free Trade Agreement. 1992. December 17. *International Legal Materials* 32: 289–456. Also available at http://nafta-sec-alena.org/english/index.htm (accessed January 2003).

Olson, Mark W. 2002. "Implementing the Gramm-Leach-Bliley Act: Two Years Later." Remarks before the American Law Institute and American Bar Association, Washington, D.C. February 8.

Organization for Economic Cooperation and Development. 2000. "Cross-Border Trade in Financial Services: Economics and Regulation." Committee on Financial Markets, Steering Group. *Financial Markets Trends* 75 (March): 23–60.

Pearson, Patrick. 2001. "EC Banking Law: General Introduction." In *Banking and EC Law: Commentary,* edited by Martijn van Empel and René Smits. Amsterdam Financial Series. Deventer, The Netherlands: Kluwer Law and Taxation Publishers.

Perreau de Pinninck, Fernando. 1993. "The Uruguay Round Financial Services Negotiations." *ECU* 24: 19–24.

Pozen, Robert G. 2002. "WTO Objectives of U.S. Asset Managers." Presentation. Conference on "Further Liberalization of Global Financial Services Markets?" Washington, D.C.: Institute of International Economics.

Roberts, Alasdair. 1999. "Access to Government Information: An Overview of Issues." Working Paper. Transparency International. Available at www.transparency.org/working_papers/roberts/robertsFOI.html (accessed January 2003).

Rogoff, Kenneth S. 2002. "Rethinking Capital Controls: When Should We Keep an Open Mind? *Finance and Development* 39 (4): 55-56.

Sachs, Jeffrey. 1998. "Global Capitalism: Making It Work." *The Economist,* September 12.

Sato, Setsuya, and John Hawkins. 2001. "Electronic Finance: An Overview of the Issues." In *Electronic Finance: A New Perspective and Challenges.* BIS Papers 7. Basel: Bank for International Settlements.

Sauvé, Pierre. 1997. "Preparing for Services 2000." Occasional Papers 4. Washington, D.C.: Coalition of Services Industries.

Securities Industry Association. 2000. "Promoting Fair and Transparent Regulation." Discussion Paper. New York: Securities Industry Association. November 8. www.sia.com./international/pdf/fair_transparent_regulation.pdf (accessed January 2003).

Skipper, Harold D., Jr. 2001. *Insurance in the General Agreement on Trade in Services.* Washington, D.C.: AEI Press.

Sorsa, Piritta. 1997. "The GATS Agreement on Financial Services—A Modest Start to Multilateral Liberalization." Working Paper 97/55. Washington, D.C.: International Monetary Fund.

Stiglitz, Joseph E. 1998. "Boats, Planes, and Capital Flows." *Financial Times,* March 25.

Summers, Lawrence H. 1998a. "Go with the Flow." *Financial Times,* March 11.

———. 1998b. "Repairing and Rebuilding Emerging Market Financial Systems." Remarks at Federal Deposit Insurance Corporation International Conference on Deposit Insurance, Washington, D.C. September 9.

Thompson, Rachel. 2000. "Formula Approaches to Improving GATS Commitments." In *GATS 2000: New Directions in Services Trade Liberalization,* edited by Pierre Sauvé and Robert M. Stern. Washington, D.C.: Brookings Institution Press.

Thompson, Rachel, and Keiya Iida. 2001. "Strengthening Regulatory Transparency: Insights for the GATS from the Regulatory Reform Country Reviews." In *Trade in Services: Negotiating Issues and Approaches,* edited by Julia Nielson and Pierre Sauvé Paris: Organization for Economic Cooperation and Development.

Treaty establishing the European Community. Consolidated Version Incorporating Changes Made by the Treaty of Amsterdam. 97/C 340/03. *Official Journal of the European Communities* 40 (C 340): 173–308 (1997). Also available at www.europa.eu.int/eur-lex/en/treaties/dat/ec_cons_ treaty_en.pdf (accessed January 2003).

United Nations Conference on Trade and Development and the World Bank. 1994. *Liberalizing International Transactions in Services: A Handbook.* New York and Geneva: United Nations.

U.S. Department of Commerce. 1990. *The Balance of Payments of the United States: Concepts, Data Sources, and Estimating Procedures.* Bureau of Economic Analysis. Washington, D.C.: U.S. Government Printing Office. Also available at www.bea.gov/bea/ARTICLES/INTERNAT/BPA/Meth/bopmp.pdf (accessed January 2003).

U.S. Department of the Treasury. 1998. "Financial Services Negotiations in the World Trade Organization." In *National Treatment Study: 1998.* Washington, D.C.: U.S. Government Printing Office.

U.S. Department of the Treasury and Board of Governors of the Federal Reserve System. 1992. *Subsidiary Requirement Study.* Report Submitted to the Banking Committees of the U.S. Senate and House of Representatives Pursuant to Section 215 of the Foreign Bank Supervision Enhancement Act of 1991.

U.S. International Trade Commission. 2001. *Recent Trends in U.S. Services Trade: 2001 Annual Report.* Pub. 3409. Washington, D.C.: U.S. Government Printing Office.

U.S. Securities and Exchange Commission. 1997. Regulation of Exchanges. Concept Release. Release 34-38672. International Series Release IS-1085. July 16. Available at www.sec.gov/rules/concept/3438672.txt (accessed January 2003).

———. 1998. Statement of the Commission regarding Use of Internet Web Sites to Offer Securities, Solicit Securities Transactions, or Advertise Investment Services Offshore. Interpretation. International Series Release No. IS-1125. March 23. Available at www.sec.gov/rules/interp/33-7516.htm (accessed January 2003).

Wang, Yi. 1996. "Most-Favoured-Nation Treatment under the General Agreement on Trade in Services—And Its Application in Financial Services." *Journal of World Trade* 30 (1): 91–124.

Wenninger, John. 2000. "The Emerging Role of Banks in E-Commerce." *Current Issues in Economics and Finance* 6 (3): 1–6. Federal Reserve Bank of New York.

Whichard, Obie G. 2001. "Measurement and Classification of Service Sector Activity: Data Needs for GATS 2000." In *Services in the International Economy,* edited by Robert M. Stern. Ann Arbor: University of Michigan Press.

White, Lawrence J. 2001. *Reducing the Barriers to International Trade in Accounting Services.* Washington, D.C.: AEI Press.

White, William R. 1998. "Promoting Financial Stability: The Role of the BIS." Paper prepared for Conference on Coping with Financial Crises in Developing and Transition Countries: Regulatory and Supervisory Challenges in a New Era of Global Finance. Amsterdam: De Nederlandsche Bank.

————. 2000. "Recent Initiatives to Improve the Regulation and Supervision of Private Capital Flows." BIS Working Papers 923. Basel: Bank for International Settlements.

Wilkinson, Ian. 1994. "The Uruguay Round and Financial Services." *Butterworths Journal of International Banking and Financial Law* 9 (6): 281–87.

Williamson, John, and Molly Mahar. 1998. *A Survey of Financial Liberalization*. Essays in International Finance 211. Princeton, N.J.: Princeton University Press.

Woolcock, Stephen. 1997. *Liberalisation of Financial Services*. London: European Policy Forum.

World Trade Organization. *Guide to Reading the GATS Schedules of Specific Commitments and the List of Article II (MFN) Exemptions.* Available at www.wto.org/english/ tratop_e/serv_e/guide1_e.htm (accessed January 2003).

————. 1995. *The Results of the Uruguay Round of Multilateral Trade Negotiations: The Legal Texts.* Reprint of 1994 volume published by the GATT Secretariat. Geneva: World Trade Organization. The legal texts are also available at www.wto.org/english/docs_e/legal_e/final_e.htm (accessed January 2003).

————. 1996a. *Technical Issues Concerning Financial Services Schedules.* Note by the Secretariat. S/FIN/W/9. July 29. Available at http://docsonline.wto.org/ (accessed January 2003).

————. 1996b. *Telecommunications Services: Reference Paper.* Negotiating Group on Basic Telecommunications. April 24. Available at www.wto.org/english/ tratop_e/serv_e/telecom_e/tel23_e.htm (accessed January 2003).

————. 1997a. *Decision Adopting the Fifth Protocol to the General Agreement on Trade in Services.* Committee on Trade in Financial Services. S/L/44. December 3. Available at http://docsonline.wto.org (accessed January 2003).

————. 1997b. *Fifth Protocol to the General Agreement on Trade in Services.* S/L/45. December 3. Available at http://docsonline.wto.org (accessed January 2003).

————. 1998a. *Financial Services: Background Note by the Secretariat.* S/C/W/72. December 2. Available at www.wto.org/english/tratop_e/serv_e/finance_e/w72.doc (accessed January 2003).

————. 1998b. *Non-attributable Summary of the Main Improvements in the New Financial Services Commitments.* Available at www.wto.org/english/news_e/ news98_e/finsum.htm (accessed January 2003).

————. 1999a. *Communication from Members which Have Accepted the Fifth Protocol to the General Agreement on Trade in Services.* S/L/67. February 15. Available at http://docsonline.wto.org (accessed January 2003).

———. 1999b. *Decision on Acceptance of the Fifth Protocol to the General Agreement on Trade in Services.* Council for Trade in Services. S/L/68. February 15. Available at http://docsonline.wto.org/ (accessed January 2003).

———. 1999c. *Procedures for the Implementation of Article XXI of the General Agreement on Trade in Services (GATS).* Council for Trade in Services. S/L/80. October 29. Available at http://docsonline.wto.org/ (accessed January 2003).

———. 2000a. *Financial Services.* Communication from the United States. Council for Trade in Services, Special Session. S/CSS/W/27. December 18. Available at http://docsonline.wto.org/ (accessed January 2003).

———. 2000b. *GATS 2000: Financial Services.* Communication from the European Communities and Their Member States. Council for Trade in Services, Special Session. S/CSS/W/39. December 22. Available at http://docsonline.wto.org/ (accessed January 2003).

———. 2000c. *Market Access in Telecommunications and Complementary Services: The WTO's Role in Accelerating the Development of a Globally Networked Economy.* Communication from the United States. Council for Trade in Services, Special Session. S/CSS/W/30. December 18. Available at http://docsonline.wto.org/ (accessed January 2003).

———. 2000d. *Procedures for the Certification of Rectifications or Improvements to Schedules of Specific Commitments.* Council for Trade in Services. S/L/84. April 18. Available at http://docsonline.wto.org/ (accessed January 2003).

———. 2001a. *Economic Needs Tests.* Note by the Secretariat. Council for Trade in Services, Special Session. S/CSS/W/118. November 30. Geneva: World Trade Organization.

———. 2001b. *Guidelines and Procedures for the Negotiations on Trade in Services.* Council for Trade in Services, Special Session. S/L/93. March 29. Available at http://docsonline.wto.org/ (accessed January 2003).

———. 2001c. *Implementation-related Issues and Concerns.* Ministerial Decision of November 14, 2001. WT/MIN(01)/DEC/17. Available at www.wto. org/english/thewto_e/minist_e/min01_e/mindecl_implementation_e.htm (accessed January 2003).

———. 2001d. *Initial Negotiating Proposal on Regulatory Transparency and Predictability.* Communication from Canada. Council for Trade in Services, Special Session. S/CSS/W/47. March 14. Available at http://docsonline.wto.org/ (accessed January 2003).

———. 2001e. *Ministerial Declaration adopted on November 14, 2001.* WT/MIN(01)/DEC/1. Available at www.wto.org/english/thewto_e/minist_e/min01_e/mindecl_e.pdf (accessed January 2003).

———. 2001f. *Transparency in Domestic Regulation.* Communication from the United States. Council for Trade in Services, Special Session. S/CSS/W/102. July 13. Available at http://docsonline.wto.org/ (accessed January 2003).

Index

About the Author

—~~~—

Sydney J. Key is on the staff of the Federal Reserve Board's Division of International Finance in Washington, D.C. In the 103rd U.S. Congress (1993–94), she was staff director of the Subcommittee on International Development, Finance, Trade, and Monetary Policy of the House Banking Committee. In 1990–91, she served as a national expert in the European Commission's Internal Market Directorate-General. Dr. Key has been a lecturer on law at Harvard Law School (2001), an adjunct professor at the Stern School of Business at New York University (1999–2000), and a lecturer at the Morin Center for Banking and Financial Law Studies at Boston University School of Law (1988–2000). She has also been an academic visitor in the Department of Accounting and Finance at the London School of Economics (1990–91). She is the author of numerous articles and studies, including *Financial Services in the Uruguay Round and the WTO* (Washington, D.C.: Group of Thirty, 1997). Dr. Key received her A.B., A.M., and Ph.D. in economics from Harvard University.

DATE DUE

MAY 0			

Demco, Inc. 38-293